Fractured Tales

Fractured Tales

Invisibles in Indian Democracy

Badri Narayan

OXFORD
UNIVERSITY PRESS

OXFORD
UNIVERSITY PRESS

Oxford University Press is a department of the University of Oxford.
It furthers the University's objective of excellence in research, scholarship,
and education by publishing worldwide. Oxford is a registered trademark of
Oxford University Press in the UK and in certain other countries.

Published in India by
Oxford University Press
YMCA Library Building, 1 Jai Singh Road, New Delhi 110 001, India

© Oxford University Press 2016

The moral rights of the author have been asserted.

First Edition published in 2016

ISBN-13: 978-0-19-946628-3
ISBN-10: 0-19-946628-9

Typeset in Adobe Garamond Pro 11/15
by The Graphics Solution, New Delhi 110 092
Printed in India by Replika Press Pvt. Ltd

No one is walking before me
No one is coming behind me
It is not as if I am the only one walking on this road for the first time
Then how am I alone?
People have walked on this road before
Today whether it is a path or a road
I have selected it
It is my fulfilled leftism*

—Dharamkirti, *Subhashitratnakosh* (1729)

* The actual word used by the poet is *vampanth* which literally means 'leftism'. However, in this poem the meaning of the word is not leftist but an uneven path that the poet has chosen; it is different from the conventional straight, simple road. In other words, the poet has chosen the path of struggle and difficulty.

Dedicated to my Babuji

Contents

Preface

Main kehta hon aankhin dekhi, tu kehta kaagad ki lekhi
(I speak what I see; you speak that is written in the books)
                                        —Saying by Kabir (Dwivedi 2008: 247)

It was around twenty to twenty-five years ago in the 1990s that I started working on dalit issues in Uttar Pradesh (UP). That was the time when the Bahujan Samaj Party (BSP) had emerged on the political scene and was gradually gaining ground in UP. Kanshiram, a *dalit* visionary, had emerged as the messiah of the dalits. A new hope was emerging in all of us that the dalits, who had been subjugated by the political parties comprising mainly of upper castes and virtually treated as captive vote banks, would get space in Indian democracy. That was when I was documenting BSP politics and was filled with enthusiasm and expectations for a bright future for dalits. The emergence of BSP was the harbinger of good tidings; the hopes that the party had instilled in the hearts of the long-suffering dalits did come true to some extent as they had begun to occupy centre stage in the political scenario of both UP and the country and could aspire for a better life due to their political empowerment. This was also the period when new liberal economic policies were being implemented in India and globalization had started spreading its tentacles in the country.

Through my fieldwork in various villages of UP at that time I was trying to understand dalit life through dalit politics. While trying to explore the relationship between dalit consciousness and politics, I developed an intimate relationship with a large number of dalit people living in several villages of UP. This intimacy was emotional but I also developed a critical eye about dalit democratic politics. I found that only a section of dalits had the power to talk about their desires, hopes, and expectations while the greater majority of the dalit communities, although now voting for BSP, continued to live in the silent zone, as they had done for many centuries. Neither did they have any visibility in dalit politics nor did they have any voice to claim the rights that BSP had provided them. Even the dalits who could speak, although they were politically aware, were still highly marginalized socially and economically. Though the image of dalits that is emerging in the prevailing political discourse of the country is that of a monolith, if someone studies dalits for a long period, one will find that the dalit subject is irretrievably heterogeneous and there exist multiple marginalities among them that are constantly being produced and reproduced.

The Bahujan Samaj Party (BSP) came to power several times in UP over the last couple of decades and gradually became an important political party at both state and national levels, but through this party too only a few dalit castes have become empowered in certain aspects. Meanwhile the rest of the dalit castes are still languishing on the fringes, far from the door of democracy. Gradually, I found that the silent zone is expanding rather than contracting after the advent of dalit politics.

I thus realized that by trying to understand dalit life through dalit politics one's vision becomes myopic. However, if we attempt to understand dalit politics through dalit life we can get a broader vision and also see politics from a larger perspective.

I started thinking to myself that this section of dalits cannot speak for themselves and the politics that had been formed for them is not giving them their voice. Other political parties are raising their issues in a very limited way because of their own self-interest and NGOs too were more concerned about getting foreign funds rather than supporting this section of dalits in their struggle for democracy. In such a situation, this issue should be raised by genuinely concerned agencies involved in the dalit struggle in order to sensitize the communities of opinion makers, politicians, and social activists. In this attempt, through the Dalit Resource Centre of the G.B. Pant Social Science Institute, Allahabad, where I am a member of the faculty, I started organizing a series of interfaces and workshops between these communities and leaders of various political parties involved in deepening democracy, writing on these issues in academic journals, publishing books on dalit issues, and contributing to newspapers and magazines in order to sensitize people at large. This book is a part of this chain and I hope it will go a long way in making general readers and policymakers aware of the plight of these marginalized and invisible dalit communities and understanding the issues facing them.

A few chapters of this book are based on ideas and research evolved in various seminar presentations and papers published in journals. I would like to acknowledge the editors of the journals and organizers of the seminars. Chapter 1 has been published as 'A Beggar's Song of Democracy: A Study of Invisible Dalits' in *Handbook of Politics in Indian States: Regions, Parties and Economic Reforms*, edited by Sudha Pai (Oxford University Press, 2013; pp. 269–80). Chapter 2, 'Is It a Snake or a Rope? Democracy and Identity Politics in India', was presented in the subaltern studies workshop on Ranajit Guha's *Elementary Aspects of Peasant Insurgency in Colonial India* (EAPI), organized by Centre for the Study of Developing Societies (CSDS), New Delhi, on 15 and 16 February 2013. I am thankful to Dipesh Chakrabarty, Gayatri Chakravarty Spivak, Gyan Pandey, Gyan Prakash, and others who were present in the workshop for their insightful comments on the paper. Chapter 3, 'Democracy, Deprivation and Dispossession: Multiple Narratives of Democracy in North India', was a special lecture delivered in the UGC Special Assistance Programme held at the Department of Political Science, Panjab University, Chandigarh from 19 to 25 August 2013. Chapter 4, 'Margins and Politics: Narratives of Marginalized Dalit Castes', was originally published as 'Domination: How the Fragments Imagine the Nation: Perspectives from Some North Indian Villages' in *Dialectical Anthropology*, vol. 29, no. 1, pp. 123–40 (New York: Springer, 2005). Chapter 5, 'With History and Without History: Dalit Reinvention of the Past', was originally published as an article, 'Demarginalisation and History: Dalit Re-Invention of the Past', in *South Asia Research*, vol. 28, no. 2, pp. 169–84 (New Delhi: Sage Publications, July 2008).

I am grateful to Professor Pradeep Bhargav, Director of the G.B. Pant Social Science Institute, Allahabad, for providing me all the support for writing this book. I would like to thank my docotoral students Rama Shankar Singh and Tarushikha Sarvesh, and my senior research assistants Ritu Sureka, Nivedita Singh, Brijendra Gautam, and Julie Khanna for helping me in various ways with this research work. I would like to thank Arindam Roy and Mousumi Majumder for translating the songs, poems, and field data from Hindi to English and also editing various chapters of the manuscript. I would also like to thank Archana Singh, faculty member of the institute, who has always provided me a great deal of support in my work. I would also like to express my gratitude to the staff of the Manav Vikas Sangrahalaya, G.B. Pant Institute, including Mr Anwar Ali, Mr Negi, and Mr Maurya, for providing infrastructural support.

Last but not least, I would like to thank my family—my father, my wife, and my daughters—for their constant moral support.

Introduction

Tracing Invisibles

Partha Chatterjee, in his book *The Politics of the Governed*, describes a political society as a site of negotiation and contestation opened up by the activities of governmental agencies aimed at population groups (Chatterjee 2004: 74). He gives the example of settlements in Kolkata (then Calcutta) that emerged in the late 1940s and gradually developed into political societies, through negotiation and contestation with various governmental agencies, to acquire the rights granted to all citizens of the nation. The settlements began with a small group of peasants who came to Calcutta from southern Bengal in search of a living after they lost their lands in the wake of the Great Famine of 1943. Several thousand others, including refugees of the Partition from East Bengal, followed these migrants and settled on public and sometimes private property in Calcutta and its suburbs. Over the years these settlements developed and flourished even though the inhabitants were most often illegal squatters on government property (Chatterjee 2004: 54).

'Political society' is the politics of subjects who wish to have the same rights as citizens, but are excluded (by dint of their very marginalization) from civil society. For the transformation of scattered people into political societies several elements are required. The first and foremost is the presence of people with leadership and organizational skills who can bring the people together under one association. The association then forms links with political parties, police, and other government agencies, on behalf of the colony (Chatterjee 2004: 54), and lays claim to a habitation and livelihood as a matter of right. Even though these settlements are on public land and are illegal, they use their association as the principal collective instrument to negotiate with the government agencies and pursue their claim.

Chatterjee's concept of 'political society' is one way of looking at marginality. Another way of looking at marginality is that of Pandey (2006: 4735) who calls marginalized castes 'subaltern citizens' but clarifies that the use of the phrase is not primarily intended to suggest the subordinate status of certain citizens though [of course] it can be used precisely to describe such a condition in particular times and places. Instead, he uses the term 'citizen' as the bearer of the legal right to residence, political participation, state support and protection in a given territory. He says that one immediate advantage of the use of the term 'subaltern citizen' is that it 'prevents the easy erection of a barrier between us (citizens, the people with history), and them (the subalterns, people without), as well as that between our times (the time of equality, democracy, the recognition of human worth) and earlier times (the time without such reason and understanding)' (Pandey 2006).

The communities which I am discussing in this book are neither political societies nor have they acquired the status of subaltern citizen as they lack 'citizenly competence' (Chakrabarty 2002: 5). Even though they exist as castes in society, they are not yet full members of the community, the village, the neighbourhood, and of the dalit community that is struggling for political and social empowerment. Most of them have not yet fully evolved as 'dalit' in the real sense.

The term 'dalit' here denotes politically assertive dalit communities whose political imagination and desire evolves around two important constituents—first, the experiences and memory of the oppression of the caste based society and second, the state which is visualized as an empowering and emancipatory agency. The languages and competencies of citizenship, of democracy and of welfare are yet to be distributed among them (Chakrabarty 2002: 33). They belong to the dalit (scheduled) castes of Uttar Pradesh (UP). Even though the dalits as a whole, who were historically highly marginalized socially, culturally, economically, and politically by the upper castes, have become politically empowered over the years after the emergence of BSP in the 1980s and 1990s, several smaller dalit castes have continued to remain scattered and fragmented and marginalized. These dalit castes, whom we call invisible dalits, are still languishing on the fringes of the dalit community and have not yet obtained political representation among the dalits a whole as they are not in a position to assert political space for themselves. Invisible dalits are produced as a result of the deepening of democracy, and as one layer after another becomes empowered, a new layer of marginality in the form of invisible dalits is produced in society. However, in this same process, through the percolation of democracy, a few invisible dalits acquire visibility and move forward politically, socially, and culturally like the other visible castes, but this process is a very slow one and can take several generations. The dalit castes that are invisible at present are unable to assert their identities in state-led democracies. In order to negotiate with the various government institutions and acquire the benefits provided by the state to marginalized communities through these institutions the disempowered communities have to acquire a language of politics that has its origins in the state. Dalit castes like the Chamar and Pasi and a few other castes that have succeeded in developing and moving ahead politically, socially, and economically have done so because of several reasons like education, creation of organic intellectuals and community leaders, and by culturally asserting their identities through their caste history, heroes, and other caste symbols. The weaker castes on the other hand are largely illiterate and have no community leaders and organic intellectuals within their castes who can mobilize them and assert their identities and stake a claim for a share in the state-led democracy.

In this book, we will discuss the reasons why a few dalit castes have succeeded in becoming politically empowered and visible while the rest of the dalit castes are lagging behind in the state-led democracy. These communities can be distinguished from the 'political' societies described by Partha Chatterjee as those communities who live in capital cities under the gaze of the camera and newspapers, and engage in political activities. Alongside, they have acquired the ways and means to make themselves politically visible in the process of their fight for existence. For political participation it is imperative to be seen and to be heard, to make the caste visible and to be articulate. The invisibility which I am describing in this book occurs as a result of the traditional as well as the newly produced caste hierarchy existing in society. The society in this case is emerging due to the contradiction of democratic politics in the process of implementation.

It is now several years since BSP (the party of the dalits) became an important and powerful political party in UP. In this process the huge dalit community of this state, which had remained socially, culturally, economically and, consequently, politically suppressed by the handful of upper castes for the last several centuries under the Brahminical order that was sanctioned by ancient Hindu religious texts, became a part of the political processes of the country. Many people feel that with the inclusion of the dalits in the country's politics, Indian democracy is now further deepening. The victory of BSP has immensely helped empower vast sections of dalits and Bahujans (the majority population) of UP who had been languishing on the fringes of democracy with no power to enter into the political processes of the country. However, in this celebration of democracy it is often overlooked that the dalits comprise a large number of castes and communities and of these only a few castes that make up a small section of the total dalit population have acquired visibility, while a huge cluster of dalit communities are still very far from the door of democracy. These castes are still invisible despite the presence of BSP and continue to remain voiceless and unable to assert themselves to move ahead. Here the term 'assert' means having a voice that matters and cannot be ignored. Voice is not merely a speech act but is a voice that can grant recognition to the speaker. It creates the capacity for intervention that might liberate the speaker and the community whom s/he represents from the conditions of invisibility (Couldry 2010: 3). Voice is needed to make us visible, not in the sense of being physically seen but in being regarded as relevant to the distribution of speaking opportunities.

The voice of a community is one which can be heard or recognized in democracy if it acquires the 'capacity' to be heard. The communities can acquire the capacity to be heard if they acquire the capacity to 'aspire' (Appadurai 2004: 64). To acquire the capacity to aspire, the communities need to attain an optimum level from where they can 'aspire' to get visibility. This capacity to aspire creates 'capacity to demand'. 'In a democracy people tend to get what they demand, and more crucially do not get what they do not demand' (Sen 1999: 156). Here the consciousness of demand and the lack of it in a democracy play a crucial role in making the visibility. However, even the voices that may get political representation might remain unheard or face denial or result in misrecognition. This may be produced by conscious denial of the communities' voices by the authorities or by misrepresentation of them in representational politics either by the state, media or by leading sections of the marginalized themselves, or by all these three. This may appear as the major limitation of representational politics in a democratic domain (Couldry 2010: 117) as they may be consciously or unconsciously eliminated or ignored by the state from being recognized as political subjects.

Communities acquire the capacity to aspire by emancipating themselves from the hurdles created by the cultural pattern and historical disabilities imposed by social systems. In this process they sometimes obtain a voice but it should be noted that it is not enough to get a voice but one should also get the value of one's voice. To attain the value of a voice, respect and recognition of the voice are needed. In the case of communities as a whole, the recognition and respect for their voice can be attained if the voiceless communities acquire confidence and strength and the power to tell in public their own story of exploitation and oppression. This symbolic location, that reproduces power in the contemporary world, might be saved from being symbolically dislocated by the narrative of the state and various other dominant social, cultural, and political authorities. The struggle to achieve symbolic power is usually done by creating their own histories, heroes, and political narratives which add in providing value to their voices. Dominant dalit castes like Chamar and Pasi, and to some extent Khatik, Kori, and Balmiki, have a large literature narrating their oppression and exploitation over the centuries, which they have successfully used to emancipate themselves and carve a space for themselves in the political and social domain of the country but, as we have mentioned earlier, there is a large section of smaller dalit castes that is still languishing on the fringes of the dalit community as a whole.

In the process of governance and in disseminating state-led democracy the state develops its own language, and the people or communities that are able to understand and respond to this language can easily get included in the state arena while those who are not able to speak or put forth their demand in that language remain excluded. However, those who are made voiceless in the domain of the state and democracy have their own language for articulating their hidden desires and aspirations which need to be recorded, documented, and analysed in order to understand them.

This book will document narratives about deepening democracy among dalits of UP, existing on the margins, whose voices have remained unheard despite the presence of BSP for more than two decades. State-led democracy has not only created empowerment but also triggered its opposite, disempowerment. The marginalized communities that gain power and get empowered wish to own all resources. They had struggled hard for their share and now they do not want to share this with their less fortunate brethren. For these excluded people, democracy and empowerment is a distant cry. In this book we examine 'how' and 'why' the process of democracy reached a small, select group amongst the dalits in UP like the Chamar and Pasi castes, while several other castes like Musahar, Bansphor, Sapera, Nat, and so on, did not even get a small glimpse of democratic empowerment. In this process, we would also like to understand their fear of growing exclusion and further marginaliza-tion as a byproduct of the project of democracy in the present form. The book will try to creatively capture their growing sense of being left out in democracy and democratic representation and their cry for inclusion, which is yet to transform into assertion in the domain of nation, state, democracy and society.

Growing Silent Zone: Understanding Invisibilities

Although 'dalit' is now almost universally preferred among research-ers and writers for the lower castes, for the lower castes 'dalit' is an imaginary entity. According to the National Family Health Survey of 1998–9, they themselves prefer to be called 'harijan' rather than 'dalit' (Marriott 2003: 3752). Officially the dalits are known as Scheduled Castes (SCs) by the government. This is a state category and SCs are given reservation in education and jobs and provided several benefits by the government, which makes it very attractive for the lower castes to claim themselves as SCs. Both the terms 'SC' and 'dalit' are homogeneous terms but while SC refers to a definite official category, dalit is an imaginary term for the lower castes and socially they prefer to be known either by their own caste names or as 'harijans'.

In the context of contemporary dalit politics, the term 'dalit' includes SC, Scheduled Tribes (STs), the so-called criminal tribes, nomadic tribes, Other Backward Classes (OBCs), and other backward social groups. These are the communities that are socially, educationally, economically, and culturally backward and have remained so for many centuries. The word 'dalit' is a recent one but the concept of dalitness is old. The term 'dalit' in Sanskrit is derived from the root *dal*, which means to split, break, crack, and so on. When used as an adjective, it means amputated, stepped on, split, broken, burst, destroyed, crushed, or ground down. Dalit implies those who have been broken and ground down by those above them in the social hierarchy, in a deliberate and active way. There is in the word itself an inherent denial, karma, pollution, and justified caste hierarchy. Dalit is a symbol of change and revolution (Zelliot 2001). According to Nandu Ram (1995), though the term dalit represents a broader social category of people, in more recent years it has become a nationwide phenomenon and is widely used by all the untouchables irrespective of traditional and parochial caste distinctions, also becoming their social identity.

The term dalit was first used by Dr Ambedkar but some sources claim that Swami Shraddhanand, a follower of the Arya Samaj, first coined it (Bechain 1997: 27). However, the etymology of the term goes back to ancient times when the dalits were known in the ancient Hindu religious texts as *shudras*, *atishudras*, *chandals*, *antyuj*, and so on. In the nineteenth century, a Marathi social reformer and revolutionary, Mahatma Jyotirao Phule, used it to describe the 'outcastes' and 'untouchables' as the 'oppressed and crushed victims of the Indian caste system'. Apparently, it was used in the 1930s as a Hindi and Marathi translation of 'depressed classes', a term the British used for what are now called the SCs. In 1930, a newspaper called *Dalit Bandhu* (Friends of Dalits) was published for the depressed classes in Pune (Bechain 1997: 98). Dr Ambedkar also used the word in his Marathi speeches. With increased sensitivity, the leaders of the Indian freedom struggle replaced it by a new term 'Harijan' coined by Mahatma Gandhi. In the cultural parlance, they were all commonly known as *achhut*, while in the legal terminology they were called 'Scheduled Castes'.

Scheduled Castes are the castes listed in the schedule by the Government of India Act, 1935. They were defined as 'such castes, races or tribes or parts or groups within castes, races or tribes, being castes, races, tribes, parts or groups, which appear to His Majesty in Council to correspond to the classes of persons formerly known as the depressed classes, as His Majesty in Council may specify' (Act 1935, First Schedule 26.i). The purpose of lists in the schedules was merely electoral, since seats in the legislative assemblies at the national and provincial levels were to be reserved for members of listed castes, and they were to form a primary electorate to choose candidates. An Indian Franchise Committee, assisted by, amongst others, the anthropologically learned Commissioner for the 1931 Census J.H. Hutton, deliberated at length over the criteria for inclusion and in particular over untouchability (Charsley and Karanth 1998: 22–3).

In UP, Chamar, Pasi, Dhobi, Khatik, Dusadh, Basor, Dhanuk, Balmiki, Kori, Dom, Gond, Kol, Dharikar, Kharwar, Musahar, Beldar, Kanjar, Nat, Bhuaiar, Ghasi, Habuda, Hari, Kalabaaz, Kapadia, Karbal, Khairaha, Agariya, Badhik, Vadi, Baiswar, Bajaria, Bajagi, Balahar, Bangali (seller of snakeskin and herbs), Bansphor, Barwar, Bedia, Bhandu, Bauriya, Korwa, Lalbegi, Mazhabi (Kahada), Parika, Paradiya, Patri, Saharia, Sansiya, Bahelia, Balai, Bawaria, and so on, are the untouchable castes included in the dalit community

Table 1.1 Marginalized Castes in UP: Their Population and Location

Caste name	Population according to the 1981 census	Areas in UP where they are found
Chamar	12,914,218	Distributed throughout the state
Pasi	3,425,929	Distributed throughout the state
Dhobi	1,423,574	Distributed throughout the state
Khatik	496,944	Distributed in almost all districts of UP
Dusadh	141,177	Distributed in the districts of Varanasi, Mirzapur, Ghazipur, Ballia, Gorakhpur, and Azamgarh
Basor	83,386	Jalaun, Jhansi, and Banda
Dhanuk	330,473	Distributed all over the state but a majority of them live in central UP
Balmiki	744,821	
Kori	1,381,588	Distributed throughout the state
Dom	55,590	Varanasi, Jaunpur, Mirzapur, Azamgarh, Ghazipur, Ballia, Deoria, Gorakhpur, Allahabad, Pratapgarh, Faizabad, and Basti
Gond	204,638	Varanasi, Mirzapur,Banda, Hamirpur, Jhansi, and Jalaun
Kol	196,654	Allahabad, Mirzapur, and Varanasi
Dharikar	58,711	Bahraich, Gorakhpur, Basti, Gonda, Azamgarh, Faizabad, Varanasi, and Allahabad
Kharwar	56,477	Varanasi, Allahabad, and Mirzapur
Musahar	126,018	Districts of central and eastern UP
Beldar	94,185	Gorakhpur, Basti, Deoria, Azamgarh, Varanasi, and Jaunpur
Kanjar	50,752	
Bhuyiar	12,635	Mirzapur, Allahabad
Habuda	3,529	Occupy the tract between the central Ganges and Jamuna Doab in UP
Hari	2,121	
Kalabaaz	5,347	

(*Cont'd*)

Table 1.1   *(Cont'd)*

Caste name	Population according to the 1981 census	Areas in UP where they are found
Kapadia	6,872	Distributed in the Bindki and Fatehpur tehsils of Fatehpur district
Karwal	12,154	Basti, Gorakhpur, Barabanki, Lucknow, and Kanpur
Khairaha Agariya	809	Mirzapur and Allahabad
Badhik	7,014	District of Muzaffarnagar and its adjoining areas
Badi/Badhi	4,472	Distributed in some parts of Saharanpur district and western UP
Baiswar	16,145	Mirzapur and Varanasi
Bajania	1,510	
Balahar	5,297	Distributed throughout UP
Bajgi	-	Distributed throughout Garhwal in UP
Bangali	31,952	Muzaffarnagar, Bijnore, and Meerut
Bansphor	18,530	Azamgarh, Gorakhpur, Ghazipur, Ballia, Varanasi, and Allahabad
Barwar	12,001	Gonda, Faizabad, Raebareli, Sultanpur, Shahjahanpur, Hardoi, and Bahraich
Bedia	19,504	Bahraich, Faizabad, Gonda, Basti, Kanpur, Barabanki, and Agra
Bhantu	6,663	Badaun district
Bauriya	4,893	Muzaffarnagar
Mazhabi	6,781	Rampur, Nainital, and Pilibhit
Sansiya	757	Meerut, Muzaffarnagar, and Moradabad
Patari	1,257	Mirzapur
Saharia	21,902	Lalitpur
Bahelia	57,470	Central and western parts of UP
Balai	1,321	Predominantly distributed in rural areas
Bawaria	4,893	Muzaffarnagar

Source: Singh (1995).

by dalit political forces. Table 1.1 shows the population of some of the marginalized castes in UP and the regions where they are mostly concentrated.

Dalits also include the STs, who are referred to in the Constitution of India as *adivasi* or original settlers. In 1931, they were given the name Scheduled Tribes after they were included in the list of communities needing special attention. In UP, the total population of STs is 22 per cent and they are mainly concentrated in Mirzapur and Sonebhadra. It should be mentioned that many of the invisible dalit castes that we are discussing in this book were earlier part of the group of Criminal Tribes notified by the colonial government—under the Criminal Tribes Act passed in 1871 by the Governor-General of India, which was amended in 1897. They were later denotified by the government of independent India in 1952.

Some people might feel that it is politically incorrect to talk about marginality within the dalit castes as it might have a deleterious effect on the growing social and political power of the entire dalit community. However, my belief is that while this kind of discussion will break the homogeneity of the dalit community and might even bring a separation at the level of discussion, when it reaches its highest peak the discussion will help to bring about political equality in these marginalized dalit castes and in the process will also make our democracy deeper and stronger. It is difficult to avoid homogeneity in the quest for making these marginalized castes more powerful. However, the homogeneity that will be formed in the process should be transitory and not permanent. Our academic, intellectual, moral, and political expectations are that someone should break the homogeneity that is being formed. This should either come from self-criticism and introspection arising from the growing political aspirations of the dominant dalit castes, or from the non-dalits who are linked with the dalit movement. It would have been better had the criticism of the growing homogeneity within the dalit castes come from dalit intellectuals as it would have enhanced both the value and acceptance of the criticism. But till it does so it is the task of non-dalit intellectuals to ensure that the voices of these marginalized dalit castes are heard and registered in the academic and intellectual discourses of the country so that they too are made visible in the politics and development of the state.

Politics of Politicizing

In this book, I would like to understand the dilemma and struggle within the entire dalit community of UP for acquiring visibility, empowerment, and political space. In this struggle only the Chamar–Pasi twins have succeeded in attaining political visibility; a few castes like the Balmiki, Dhobi, and Koris are fighting to attain visibility, while a large number of smaller castes are still completely marginalized and not even present in this discourse. Although there are several reasons for the invisibility of the large number of smaller and marginalized dalit castes, the major reasons for their multiple invisibility are the absence of their own leadership and consequently their not developing a modern politics of their own; absence of education and literacy among them which has led to paucity of intellectuals, writers, and journalists who can write and spread information about them and increase their visibility; the small numbers and scattered form of their population due to which they are unable to conglomerate and make their presence felt during elections; their incapacity to mould their identity in the modern language of politics and power, and so on. This category of people can be found in almost all states of the country but their status and condition differs from state to state. For example in Kerala, dalits, tribals, and coastal communities were recognized early enough as deserving welfare endowments and paternal care of the state (Devika 2013: 10).

These most marginalized communities are indeed dalits by category but due to lack of agency are constative, not performative. The lack of agency is caused by certain conditions such as elements of historical deficit in their progress, lack of education, lack of community leaders for responding to modern democratic politics, and so on. They are in a stage where they cannot represent themselves; they must be represented as Marx observed for classes who lack class consciousness. While talking of class formation Marx said that there are two ways in which the same group of people are and are not a class, depending upon whether they have a consciousness of class. While talking about small peasant proprietors in France he wrote, 'They cannot represent themselves; they must be represented,' and added, 'They are therefore incapable of asserting their class interest in their own name' (Marx, trans. from German to English by David Fernbach, 1992: 239).

Distinct from the dalit castes of UP, those of south India are highly assertive and there is constant conflict among themselves for grabbing a larger share of benefits. For example, there is growing competition among dalit castes like the Malas, Madigas, Adi-Andhra, Rellis, and so on, for reservation benefits. Scheduled Caste reservations have not reached the SCs equally, resulting in differential development among them. This has led to caste differences among them, and the less-benefitted segments are now demanding justice and equality. One such caste is the Madiga of Andhra Pradesh, which has successfully organized the Dandora Movement demanding a just share in the SC reservation system. The Madigas are the most populous among the 60 SCs in Andhra Pradesh of which the other major castes are Mala and Adi Andhra. Malas and Madigas are in constant rivalry and the Malas consider the Madigas inferior to them. The Malas have benefitted more and are far ahead of Madigas as regards educational and occupational status. In fact they are ahead of all other SCs. Traditionally, the Madigas used to tan leather and worked as village servants, known as Tettivadu, while the traditional occupation of the Malas was weaving.

The Madigas used to beat 'dappulu', also called 'dandora', which was the reason behind naming their movement the Dandora Movement. The Madiga Dandora Movement was led by the Madiga Reservation Porata Samiti (MRPS), started by about 20 Madiga youths, on 27 July 1994 in Eadumudi village of Prakasam district, who had gauged the general discontent among the Madigas over the apportioning of reservation benefits. MRPS demanded their just share in the present quota based on their population. The movement was successful because of its strategy, leadership, and ideology. It was largely non-political, and the MRPS leaders never tried to hurt the feelings of the Malas while expressing the injustice done to the Madigas.

Another feature of the Dandora Movement was the success in enhancing the self-respect and social profile of the Madigas. They organized the Madigas by identifying and glorifying their own traditional caste symbols, norms, and values. The strategy of using their caste symbols like the 'dappulu' in their public rallies and using terms like Madiga and Dandora to refer to their movement was highly successful; it hinted to the higher castes that they could no longer verbally abuse the Madigas and that the latter would no longer endure such humiliation submissively. The fight helped advance the cause of justice for other backward SCs like the Rellis and so on too. The success of the Dandora Movement has also helped the backward STs to organize the Thadum Movement demanding classification of ST reservations (Venkata Siva Reddy 2002).

It thus needs to be noted that both in north and south India the dalit castes that have progressed are unwilling to share their democratic, political, and socio-economic opportunities and their resources with these marginalized dalit castes, and also that these marginalized dalit castes are yet to aspire for their basic rights and visibility. In addition, in some parts of India the phenomenon of horizontal discrimination exists in which the lower sub-castes of dalits are socially discriminated against by higher sub-castes of dalits. In a joint long-term study of 1,589 villages of Gujarat by the Navsarjan Trust and the Robert F. Kennedy Center for Justice and Human Rights (2009) it was found that there exist several forms of horizontal discrimination, the most common being the prevention of lower sub-caste dalits from sitting with the rest of the dalit community during special meals. This food-related discrimination is directly parallel to the most prevalent vertical discrimination between non-dalit and dalit castes that requires dalits to bring plates from home to prevent 'defilement' of the non-dalits. The study found various other forms of horizontal discrimination like not serving water to lower sub-castes of dalits in the homes of higher dalit sub-castes. Another form of vertical discrimination was that people belonging to lower dalit sub-castes are not allowed to sit with upper sub-caste dalits in activities like *katha* (religious discourses). In addition, not only are they not allowed to touch items used for religious rituals, but are also not permitted to participate in the inauguration of temples; nor are they allowed to enter temples of Madh, the chief goddess of the higher dalit sub-caste. Finally, the *prasad* or holy food is usually thrown into the palm of the lower sub-caste dalits so that there is no physical touch with them. All these practices parallel the vertical discrimination between non-dalits and dalits.

Along with the social discrimination that these castes face within the dalit community as a whole, they are totally invisible in the Indian state and its welfare schemes. Dalit history and dalit culture in totality are marginalized to a great extent in our country's policies and academic discourses but even within these the history and culture of the marginalized dalit castes are completely absent. The future of the Indian state is completely dependent on how far these marginalized dalit castes are politicized and modernized within the Indian state. As these marginalized dalit castes become politically aware and are able to knock on the doors of democracy, Indian democracy will become stronger and deeper. Many of these original dalit castes are the victims of confusion between how they will negotiate their traditional occupations with the language of the modern state, and what position they will take regarding education and modern forms of marketing. Their traditional occupations are declining but because they are not familiar with the language and politics of the state they are unable to make themselves visible in the democratic domain. The government too has never carried out a special drive to include them in its homogeneous kind of politics in order to reach out to them. They are not in the radars of the forces that form the political policies and academic discourses of the country and have not yet been able to haunt their mindspaces. In addition, these marginalized dalit castes have not entered into the mainstream discourse through education and no desire for education has arisen within the marginalized castes that will take them to the existing schools in their region. Due to this absence of an educated and political group within these castes no agency has emerged to translate the state welfare schemes into a language understood by them, whether it is in their own language or in a language that will be easily understood by them.

When Kanshiram emerged on the socio-political scenario of India, he positioned himself as a leader of all the dalits as a whole and tried to create a homogeneous dalit identity for all the diverse dalit castes that comprise the lower castes of the Indian social system by providing respect to the identity of each and every dalit caste and striving to provide representation to them in the democratic power set-up. Kanshiram also included the OBCs in his definition of dalit. He termed the SCs, STs, OBCs, Nomadic, and backward castes together as the 'Bahujan Samaj'. OBCs are those castes that occupy an intermediary position in the Hindu caste hierarchy. Economically and socially they were as backward as the untouchables but their 'touch' was not polluting for the upper castes. They could thus work as servants in their households. This led these castes to identify them-selves more with the upper castes than with the untouchables and to keep away from them. This feeling of superiority historically has been the reason for the schism between them and the untouchables. But after the implementation of the Mandal Commission Report granting protective discrimination to the SCs, the OBCs and the BCs, a unity was forged between the dalits and the OBCs against the upper castes during the anti-Mandal movement (Navsarjan Trust and the Robert F. Kennedy Center for Justice and Human Rights 2009). At that time a large chunk of the OBCs joined hands with the BSP and started relating themselves to the Dalits. Some important OBC castes of UP are Kewat, Tewar, Garariya, Kahar, Nai, Mali, Bhar, Rajbhar, Bind, and Kanera (Prasad 1995: 72). The BCs are the castes that lie above the OBCs but are lower than the upper castes in the caste hierarchy. They believe that the people of these castes were originally Brahmins and Kshatriyas who were declared social outcasts under the strict social and cultural code of conduct. As a result, many of them add the middle name 'Singh' to signify their affinity with the upper castes. Although the BSP in UP is trying hard to bring the backward castes under their fold, they prefer to link themselves with the SP. The Ahirs (Yadavs), Gujars, Kurmi, Lodhi, Kumhar, Darzi, Lohar, and Sonar are some of the major backward castes of this region (Prasad 1995).

Democratizing Democracy

In UP, the SCs comprise 21 per cent of the total population of the state. Of this the Chamars make up the largest percentage—55. The Pasi is the next-largest community, with a population of nearly 34,25,929. Dhobi, Kori, Balmiki, Shilpkar, Khatik, and Dhanuk are the other numerically important dalit castes in the state (Prasad 1995: 20). These few numerically strong castes have succeeded in taking advantage of the BSP-led dalit movement, while the invisible and unseen communities amongst the dalits are unable to demonstrate their politics of presence in the ever-evolving democracy of UP and are still far from the threshold of democracy. Thus, while the state-led democracy has helped to empower many erstwhile marginalized communities, it has also led to the disempowerment of many other small communities. The marginalized communities that have gained power do not want to share it with less fortunate brethren, thus creating a dominant community. The Chamar caste, which is the largest dalit caste, has emerged as one of the most dominant castes among them. There were several reasons for this, the chief reason being the spread of education among them during the colonial period which enabled many of them to get jobs in cities and transform themselves into a political caste after Independence. This helped in the making of an intelligentsia and community leaders which began with the emergence of the middle class. When Kanshiram emerged on the scene he thus found a readymade cadre for the party in its initial phase. Thus a major chunk of the BSP was made up of cobbler caste cadre that succeeded in cornering the benefits of dalit political empowerment because of their urge to move ahead.

However, many other dalit castes like Jogi, Musahar (who make items out of leaves), Dom, Domar, Hela (who work as sweepers), Basor (who weave baskets), and so on, that in spite of being in good-numbers are so insignificant overall that they cannot create an impact on vote-bank politics; they thus continue to face exclusion. Apart from the mentioned castes, there are still many other dalit castes found in fewer numbers like the Bahelia (who hunt birds); Khairaha (who work as woodcutters); Kalabaaz (who sing songs and perform acrobatics); Balai (who work as farm labourers); Majhwar (who play musical instruments); Hari (who make baskets); Sansiya (who repair musical instruments); Kuchbadiya/Patharkatwa (who cut stones for making idols, grinding stones for domestic use, and so on); Sarvan/Kankhutwa (who take wax out of people's ears); Madari/Sapera (who catch snakes in the jungle and, in urban areas, from the homes of people); Kol (who collect firewood and leaves from the forest and sell these at the local markets); Bansphor (also known as Banbasi, who make bamboo furniture); Chamarmangta (also known as Nona Chamar, who seek alms, cut stones, and so on); *Nat*-Kanjar (who sell their handmade items or sell and buy animals and also entertain people by walking on ropes, wrestling, and so on); Nat (who buy and sell animals and also seek alms); Mahavat (a nomadic caste who work as elephant-tamers, tenders, and riders).

Even though these castes are in a highly marginalized condition today it is worth mentioning that several of them were very prominent during the 1857 Rebellion; they played active roles in it since it was more of a people's movement (Narayan 2006: 48). However, over the years, the condition of these castes deteriorated as other castes, especially the castes above them in the social hierarchy who were more privileged started acquiring education and became visible and prominent. During the nationalist movement these castes remained sidelined and because they were steeped in illiteracy and poverty were completely obliterated from Indian mainstream social history since there was no one in their community who was literate and aware and could write their caste histories or about their caste heroes. In the decade of the 1960s when the literate and conscious dalit castes like the Chamars and Pasis that had taken advantage of education during the colonial period, started writing their caste histories, and asserting their identities through their 'glorious past' these invisible castes were unable to do so. Thus they could not consolidate their caste members under their caste identity and remained scattered and disintegrated. We recently surveyed a few of them and found that each was totally fragmented and lacking in unity. These highly marginalized dalit castes are not even at the minimum economic level of production where they can develop their own politics and also their 'organic' intellectuals who, according to Gramsci, every new class creates alongside itself and who direct the ideas and aspirations of the class to which they organically belong (Hoare and Smith 1996: 5). According to Gramsci, every social group, coming into existence on the original terrain of an essential function in the world of economic production, creates together with itself, organically, one or more strata of intellectuals which gives it homogeneity and an awareness of its own function not only in the economic but also in the social and political fields. These organic intellectuals are important for the development of a caste since they are literate and can translate the language of the state into a language easily understood by the rest of the members of the caste. The state develops its own language for ruling, and those people or communities that are literate and are able to decipher this language are easily included in the statistics of the state. On the other hand, those who are unable to place their demands in the language of the state are neglected and isolated and their voices remain unheard. This disconnect between them and the state can be understood from the words of Lalchand,[1] belonging to the Musahar community who lives in Anai village near Banaras. He says, *Bhaiya ye jo upar wale (officers and political leaders) log aate hain, ya to hamare baat sunte nahin, sunte hain to theek se samajhte nahin, samajhte hain to ulta hi karte hain* (Bhaiya, either the officers and political leaders who come here do not listen to us, if they hear they do not understand us, and if they do understand they do just the opposite). From this statement one can gauge the level of disconnect between the subalterns and the state and political elites.

If we base our argument on Bourdieu's (1990) concept of how culture affects poverty and the reproduction of inequality, as interpreted by Rao and Walton (2004: 15), these castes are positioned so low in the Hindu caste hierarchy that they lack the habitus, which can be thought of as the set of durable principles in the form of practices, beliefs, taboos, rules, representations, rituals, symbols, and so on that provide a group of individuals with a sense of group identity and consequent feelings of security and belongingness. These culturally produced dispositions, beliefs, and behaviours in the habitus tend to shape individual action so that existing opportunity structures are perpetuated and while they create an acceptance of hierarchy among the higher castes they also work as social sanctions for individuals from lower castes who engage in class struggle. Thus, according to Bourdieu, culture is also a form of capital and the absence of the cultural capital of the upper castes among the marginalized dalit castes limits their aspirations, creates discrimination, and blocks mobility. Bourdieu further says that in addition to culture, individuals and groups can also draw upon their social and symbolic resources to maintain and enhance their position in the social order. According to Bourdieu, social capital emphasizes the social networks available to people to access and mobilize resources and contributes to inequality because elites are able to access internal and external social networks that are more powerful and wealthy. By contrast the poor have less influential networks that, although helping them to cope with the vicissitudes of life, restrict their chances for mobility. Different groups within a social system can have different types of social capital, and because they can be bequeathed, they play an important role in the reproduction of inequality. They are contextualized because they commingle with habitus and cultural capital. They can be used for constructive purposes—not only to facilitate collective action or to improve economic productivity but also for destructive purposes by perpetuating symbolic or actual violence (Rao and Walton 2004: 16).

Because of this absence of social and cultural capital of the upper castes that leads to the absence of voice among the marginalized dalit castes, they need an outside agency to speak for them. But if any attempt is made from the outside to ameliorate their condition by granting them collective speech, it often leads to a logocentric assumption of cultural solidarity among a heterogeneous people, and there emerges a dependence upon western intellectuals to 'speak for' the subaltern condition rather than allowing them to speak for themselves (Spivak 1988: 286). Often the leading sections speak for the dalit community as a whole, according to their interpretation of the aspirations of the groups and castes constituting it. This articulate section works as an agency to link the communities with the state in the process of their empowerment in order to translate the state policies and programmes to the marginalized communities and also to create pressure on the state and give visibility to the communities. This agency provides visibility to the communities by writing about them in newspapers, forming caste associations, writing their caste histories, and so on. However, this section sometimes becomes an 'other' of the community as it starts acquiring elite desires and forms a kind of creamy layer.[2] In this condition, sometimes there are dangers of misrepresentation and dislocated symbolic identities. This misrepresentation of the voiceless sections by the articulate sections of dalits, both of their own caste and other smaller castes, often creates metanarratives that produce greater invisibilities in the long run. Sometimes the state and its authorities encourage such misrepresentations and approve the demands of the articulate sections. This kind of misrepresentation followed by misrecognition creates a picture in which a few castes become visible while many others appear hazy and invisible in the catalogue of democracy. This process is inevitable in the evolution all communities but especially in the case of marginalized communities and it is through this process that consciousness trickles down to the grassroots and a critical section develops within the community that works as a watchdog for the cluster of the leading section. However, this is a lengthy process and in the meantime other agencies not directly linked to these communities by birth like NGO and social movement activists, academics and, sometimes, political parties provide inputs from outside to develop the communities. The state also works as an agency for granting them welfare schemes and developing the communities but often the officials are unable to understand the particular demands of the different castes and grant them homogeneous schemes that are not appropriate for the caste.

The existence of this marginalized group among the dalits is now being recognized and another group called *ati-dalit* (lowest of the low) has been created as a result of this exclusion. This group has now become visible to various political parties and the Congress Party in its election manifesto for the UP Assembly elections had promised to give respect, representation, and status to these castes in UP. The Samajwadi Party, currently ruling the state did not, however, address this most marginalized of the marginalized groups in its election manifesto or governance policies. As the Congress Party did not win the elections in UP and Kanshiram is also not alive to fight for the rights of the marginalized dalit castes, the ati-dalits of UP continue to remain marginalized in this state. In the neighbouring state of Bihar, Chief Minister Nitish Kumar created a new category called *Mahadalits* after observing the phenomena of exclusion amongst the dalit communities in Bihar. Although this move was seen by political analysts and his opponents as a vote-bank stratagem, it does have the merit of registering the fact of social exclusion among the dalits.

When Nitish Kumar appointed Jitin Ram Majhi, a member of the very low dalit Musahar caste as chief minister of Bihar it was seen as a political move but in this process the Musahars have obtained a foothold in the political processes of the country. Another example is Bhagvati Devi, the first-ever woman Musahar MLA in Bihar. With the entry of some members of the Mahadalit and ati-dalit castes in Bihar and UP into the democratic processes of the country these castes will be able to gain political empowerment through the trickle-down effect but this process is a very long one and will depend on the presence of organic intellectuals able to arouse awareness and consciousness among the members of these communities and instil in them the desire to progress through education and political empowerment.

It bears noting that the genesis of the problem of the margins in the process of disseminating democracy to dalits lies in Kanshiram's notion of 'Bahujan power'. He had tried to mobilize dalit communities based on the slogan, *jiski jitni sankhya bhari, uski utni sajhedari* (the greater the numbers you have, the bigger the share in power structure). This notion, based on the size of population of a particular caste, has led to the dominance of the numerically greater communities in the long run. Hence the bigger castes got the leverage of power while those fewer in number were marginalized from the democratic processes despite their efforts. In this process democracy is actually going into the hands of those forces hurting democratic values by their dominance and creating hurdles in distribution of democratic resources among the most marginalized of the marginalized. It goes against the logic of 'representation of particulars' which demands that each social group be represented (Tanabe 2007: 565). The dalit castes that are large numberwise and have taken advantage of the process of political empowerment and have moved ahead socially and culturally, are not concerned with the plight of the smaller dalit castes that have been left behind in this process. Big and major dalit castes like the Pasis, Chamars, Koris, and so on who can struggle politically against the atrocities and violence committed on small and vulnerable dalit castes by upper and OBC castes, do not come out in the support of these castes although they belong to the same bigger group of dalits. An incident that occurred recently in a small village called Pakaha, 45 kilometres from the district headquarters of Deoria in eastern UP, adjacent to district Gopalganj in Bihar, supports this observation. The village is sited in about 20 bighas of land and is mostly inhabited by various dalit communities such as manual scavengers, Bansphors, and so on. Suresh Bansphor of this village makes baskets at his hut; it does not even fetch him Rs 100 a day. Once he slashed his face while cutting a bamboo cane and needed immediate medical attention. He went to the local doctor who did not treat him under some pretext or other.[3]

Another incident occurred on 3 July 2010, at the Sheetalpur Tikari village under Tharwai police station only 30 kilometres from Allahabad town around 8 am. Lalli Devi, a poor 45-year-old woman of the Dharikar caste that is involved in bamboo weaving faced an attempt to rape by the dominant Brahmin caste. Her clothes were torn and the miscreants tried to urinate into her mouth. She, her husband Gulab, and her son aged 12 years, were beaten mercilessly and their hut razed. But the police kept her in the police station for 24 hours and tried to deny that any such thing had happened. The village has five families of Yadavs, 10 families of Patels (OBCs), 25 to 30 families of Pasis (dalits) and nearly 20 families of Brahmins. Nearly 10 families belong to Telis, that is, Guptas, and there is just one Dharikar family and it bears the worst brunt of the caste system in the village. None of the communities came to Lalli Devi's rescue. The Kurmis, a powerful OBC, did not respond, nor did the Pasis who are otherwise known to resist. 'Most people saw me being dragged along the ground and my clothes being torn but nobody stirred as they fear the powerful,' said Lalli Devi.[4]

The most marginal of the marginalized need to acquire visibility, which is possible only by acquiring the capacity to aspire and then translate aspiration into reality through the means followed by other dalit castes. These lesser dalit groups need to counter their disembodiment and to do that they need to develop their own politics. The dominant dalit groups that now have control over the scarce resources should act as agencies to help distribute them to the poorest of the poor rather than gobble them up themselves. In fact, for dalit politics to be sharp and dynamic it is necessary that all smaller and lesser dalit groups that are now invisible and unseen, are included within its socio-political matrix.

Negotiating with State-led Democracy in India

Following Homi Bhabha (1994) there are two models of democratic politics in the world. One is the pedagogic model and the other is the performative model. In the pedagogic model a citizen is produced at the end of an educational process at schools, colleges, or universities. Citizenship is based on the capacity for reasoning (Chakrabarty 2002: 7). In the performative model the acquisition of citizenly rights is not conditional on any preparatory work on behalf of the people (Chakrabarty 2002: 6). This debate was present in several countries of the world, for example in Australia in the 1940s it was advocated that only the 'civilised Aboriginals' were fit for citizenship (Chakrabarty 2002: 6). In the decade of the 1960s, however, all the Aboriginals were granted citizenship whether they were educated or not. The same debate occurred in India also at the attainment of Independence, which was whether to adopt universal adult franchise as a citizenly right in a society that was predominantly non-literate. It was ultimately decided to adopt universal adult franchise and grant each citizen the right to vote whether he or she was literate or not. As the world became more and more politicized and several social movements and cultural wars took place globally in the last century, the pedagogic model could not keep pace with the changes; the theoretical debate had to be shelved and the performative model of political democracy now functions in all democracies of the world.

In India, which is the world's largest democracy, the one achievement that is usually highlighted about democracy is the growing sense of empowerment and breaking the shackles of marginalization by the weaker sections of the society. However, we often miss the fact that empowerment and marginalization sometimes go together, sometimes side by side, at times supplementing each other or countering each other, with the cases varying for the communities that are competing for development in democracy. So marginalization appears in our everyday life in both ways—it is real and constructed.

In its constructed form it evolves and develops in the context of state-led democracy, which appears as a resource-distributing and opportunity-providing agency. This can be understood from the narratives of marginalization of different communities which show how the state-led democracy works as the central locus of identity construction of social groups in our society. It is interesting to observe that these narratives of marginalization mostly emerge as critical and complaint-based against democracy, since these are based on the aspiration and desire for a better life of the marginalized communities.

In the Indian context, the state is perceived as the primary instrument of delivering democracy. During our fieldwork in northern Indian villages, especially in UP, we observed that in popular parlance state and democracy are being perceived as synonymous with each other. Both state and democracy are understood by the rural people in their everyday life as 'sarkar'. The idea of *sarkar* (government) in vernacular life is rather different from the European meaning of government that is perceived as rational governing agency. It means government and powerful people (*huzoor*, modern masters or political leaders—*neta*, powerful people, who may or may not directly be part of the government but attain power in the corridors of the state), who all run the government directly and indirectly or the *sarkar banane ke liye chunav* (election politics to enter government).[5] This sarkar in its combined meaning of state and democracy invokes a lot of undirected and uncontrollable social aspiration despite the 'global dominance of ideas of liberalization' (Kaviraj 2005: 2). Sudipto Kaviraj rightly observed that 'there is no end in sight of the Indian society's strange enchantment with the modern state' (Kaviraj 2005). This very enchantment may be one of the causes of the enormous rise of dissatisfaction against the state and state-led democracy.

This is a very peculiar situation for democracy in Indian society, especially in villages in north India. While observing the working of state-led democracy in villages it sometimes appears that no one seems to be satisfied with democracy. All the people we talked to had a large number of complaints against state-led democracy. The major complaint was that the government was not doing anything for them. Both the relatively rich and the poor had similar narratives in the context of state-led policies and development aimed at strengthening and deepening democracy. There may be two reasons for this. First, they felt that the person asking questions might be a government official and so they deliberately exaggerated the intensity of their problems in the hope of getting some benefits. Second, the state-led democracy, in its present form, has given rise to a great deal of expectations among the people, which they express in the form of deprivations.

However, when we dug deeper into the psyche of the people through long-term interviews, we found that some presence of state-led development and democracy is found in each person's life even though it is never sufficient and satisfies none. State-led democracy in India reinvented various methods to fulfil the urges and desires of communities and deepen democracy at the grassroots. Forming categories as a technique of managing democracy appeared as one of the modes of delivering protective discrimination to provide support and benefit of democracy to the weaker sections of the population. To deepen democracy and attack the caste system, the Indian Constitution, along with other measures like the abolition of the caste system, formed a system of reservation based on these categories in three sectors—electoral representation, government employment and educational institutions (Kaviraj 2005: 13).

These categories linked with census and numbering play an important role in governance. While exploring the politics of category-making Ian Hacking (1975) and Arjun Appadurai (1993) said that numbers were elegant, discrete, comparable, and meaningful within and across categories and units. Dirks also reconstructed the meaning of numbers and said numbers could be used to generate information concerning the caste composition of discrete areas of imperial control in relation to military recruitment, police control, land settlement operations, market intervention, and legal policy (Dirks 2002: 199–200). These categories were formed by the colonial governance for population counting but later on they were used for protective discrimination and electoral mobilization.

This reinvention of categories later evolved as a powerful tool during democratic elections of electoral mobilization of marginal communities in India like the SCs, STs, and OBCs. The demands for shifting categories by upper, middle, and lower castes are the outcome of their growing sense of marginalization in the allotted state location and the hope of coming out from it by changing state-created categories.[6] In governance, these categories are considered homogeneous entities but in reality they contain multiple forms of heterogeneities and various layers of social locations for these castes.[7]

It is interesting to observe that sometimes during electoral mobilizations, political parties and the media believe that these categories work well as they help mobilize a larger percentage of voters in favour of certain political parties. It is only when the distribution of democratic resources takes place that these heterogeneities, stories of marginalization, and narratives of dispossession become visible. Hope for a better future binds them all together. All groups, big and small, come together for a common cause. A case in point is the Mandal Commission agitation, when even smaller groups of OBCs and SCs rallied together for common gains such as government jobs, housing, and other development policies aimed at strengthening the weaker sections and providing equitable social justice within the target group. This was the dream that was shown to these marginalized communities by the ruling political party. But the reality was harsher, perhaps more cruel than the dreams. The desire of the dominant and vocal sections of these categories to take more share of the resources resulted in an inequitable distribution of resources based on caste. This situation created competition among the different marginalized castes at various levels with the smaller and less powerful being left out of the share of the resources. These communities now want to shift to other categories as they believe that they will get more benefits in this way. The trend among them is to try to shift to lower state-created categories as they feel that these categories are being given more benefits by the government. The ruling political party and other parties use these desires that emerge from the deprivation of these communities for strengthening their base among the respective communities.

Even political parties support the demand of communities to move to lower categories as can be seen by the fact that the Samajawadi Party (SP) government, in UP, is in the process of sending its recommendations to the Centre for including 17 OBCs in the SC category. These castes are Kahar, Kashyap, Kewat, Machuwa, Mallah, Nishad, Kumhar, Prajapati, Dheevar, Bind, Bhar, Rajbhar, Biyar, Batham, Gond, and Tairaha. The SP had included these castes in the SC category by managing to intrude in the Centre's rights to change quotas and categories. The SP sources accused previous chief minister and BSP chief, Mayawati, of protecting her political interests by depriving these castes of their rights. Under Mulayam Singh Yadav's government, in October 2005, a government order was passed, providing facilities on a par with SCs to these 17 most-backward OBCs. This move of Yadav was stayed by the Allahabad High Court following a writ filed by the BSP. After Mayawati became CM, she withdrew the recommendations of the previous SP government and quashed them on 6 June 2007.[8] But, before quashing the previous government, Mayawati urged the Centre to increase the SC reservation quota by another eight per cent before these 17 castes were to be included. However, all these recommendations have a vested political interest as SP sources opined that these 17 castes that constitute 15 per cent of the total population of UP were capable of changing the forthcoming Lok Sabha election results in favour of the

SP. Mayawati feared her defeat and thus withdrew the proposal sent by the SP government earlier.[9]

Indifferent to the vested interests of the political parties a strong tussle emerged among many middle and most backward castes to be included in the government and state-created low categories. This is because of the benefits of reservations and quotas that the lower categories enjoy now which translate into assured government jobs. While some OBCs wish to acquire SC status, a section of SCs like Musahar, Nat, Kanjar, Bansphor, and so on are demanding inclusion in the ST category, as they feel that the STs are given more benefits by the government. These small dalit groups reasoned that some big and influential castes within the SC category had usurped all the benefits meant for the entire section. Being small, insignificant and not vocal, by the time their turn came, every benefit was taken away by the bigger, powerful, and dominant dalit castes and they were left empty-handed. This problem is being faced by 62 of the 66 castes among dalits in UP which are small in number. The Musahars have a population of 10 lakh but each of the castes such as Dusadh, Bansphor, Kanjar, Kharvar, Bhuiar, Dom, Nat, Bahelia, Kalabaaz, Pankha, and so on is less than two lakh.

Not only is the population size of these castes small, the literacy level among them is also very low. Very few youths among them have progressed beyond the intermediate stage. Many of these castes are engaged in traditional vocations and they have neither diversified nor modernized their caste-based professions. The benefits of government schemes do not reach them because they are not educated and also lack political leadership. Thus, they are unable to make their presence felt in the discourses and debates within the SCs, and are largely invisible. State government officials like District Magistrates (DMs), Sub-district Magistrates (SDMs), and Block Development Officers (BDOs), who are responsible for protecting and developing these castes are not even aware about them. In the neighbouring

Kaushambi district, one of the state government officials whom we interviewed was not aware that just a couple of kilometres away from his official residence there was a settlement of Musahars.

These aspirations of the small dalit caste were made vocal in a recent conference held at Barahi Navada, near Varanasi, on 26 November 2012 in which the leaders of some of these small dalit castes met to discuss their problems. Another meeting was held at Fatehpur, on 12 February 2013, while a third meeting was held at the Ganga Prasad Memorial Hall, Lucknow, on 7 March 2013, where caste leaders of nine SC groups, from Bhadohi, Jaunpur, Varanasi, Allahabad, Kaushambi, Fatehpur, Unnao, Barabanki, Lucknow, and Lalitpur met and handed over a memorandum to the state government to press their demands for inclusion in the ST category instead as they felt that the change in category would help them get jobs in anganwadis, gain access to various health schemes and get the benefits of reservation—things that have eluded them so far.

Cultural Citizenship, Dalits, and the Indian Nation: Relating Culture and Desires

The meaning of space in democracy is not just limited to providing political representation and economic development to all the communities but also includes providing space to their cultural identities including their dialect. This can be done by giving respect to their cultural forms by encouraging and supporting them and documenting their language and dialect. However, the state often attempts to appropriate the cultural forms of the different communities of the country and tries to homogenize them and manipulate and plan a national culture, but then it forgets that it will be no longer culture, since if culture cannot be seen or experienced in disjunction from life, the question of its control or planning does not arise (Nagendra 2012: 137). This process might also diminish the cultural autonomy of the various communities which consider themselves part of the nation. In a state-led democracy all the communities try to acquire visibility and attain cultural citizenship, which helps them to be elevated in the eyes of other castes and get social respect. Cultural citizenship depends on a sense of identity and cultural 'ownership' of each community and extends an invitation to the communities to belong and become a part of the democracy. Cultural citizenship is only realized when there is a sense of authenticity and connection. Sometimes this translates into belonging, and only then is there a recognizable citizenship structure that includes rights and responsibilities. Although such a practice is highly relevant to citizenship in a general sense, as it bonds groups of people and bridges significant differences and may, at times, have political impact far beyond its original domain, it remains primarily a cultural practice and often a temporary involvement for individuals. Cultural citizenship itself should not be naively taken to supplant or even be as important as the primarily political and social rights of the other citizenships (Hermes and Adolfsson 2007: 1).

Culture has multiple connotations that mean different things to different people. For some it is the exploration of the self (Coomaraswamy 2006), while for others it is a representation of the everyday life of common people, reflecting the desires and dreams of their particular community. It is also a vehicle for carrying a community's collective memories through time and space. According to the Human Development Report (2004: 88), culture was for long perceived as a homogeneous, coherent, stable, and bounded whole, but over the past two decades it has been revaluated by theorists and anthropologists as a site of difference, multiplicity, contest, negotiation, and also a domain of power and authority discourse. Earlier, culture was managed by the communities themselves and grew and developed with the life of the people by interacting with various kinds of influences. The new notions around culture, however, linked

with development, managing identity and cultural freedom in mul-
ticultural societies like India, extend the meaning of culture to being
a state-oriented idea, notion and site (Rao and Walton 2004: 9).
National and global forces assert themselves in determining and defining the politics of cultural practices in the contemporary context, and
these practices largely appear as attempts of conscious mobilization
of cultural differences in service of larger national or transnational
politics (Appadurai 1997: 15). Since culture reconstructs the subjec-
tivity of the people and in the process transforms and changes them,
when used and controlled by the state it is a powerful tool to govern
the people as a vital step towards nation-building. Culture is used by
the state not only to contain 'national crises' but also to justify the
state's legitimacy in governing culture as part of nation-building. For
this purpose, cultural institutions and establishments are created and
maintained by the state. They are entrusted with the responsibility of
furthering a composite or national culture. However, these institutions' selection of cultural traditions to encourage and nurture has a
definite politics behind it, which often results in a vertical growth of
culture dictated by the state and the market at the cost of a horizontal
growth that provides space to all communities and promotes a genu-
ine 'people's culture'.

India, with its multilayered, heterogeneous and fragmented social
structure is characterized by an enormous multiplicity of cultures due
to the close association of culture with the everyday socio-economic
life of its people and communities. 'While discussing the cultural
policies of India it is thus necessary to view its complex, intricate and
multilayered, multidimensional cultural fabric, which is a reflection
of the stratified social fabric of the country. This cultural diversity is a
continuity which has survived through 5,000 years of history marked
by periods of unrest, invasions, war, political subjugation, economic
underdevelopment and has conditioned, guided and governed the
value system of a whole people, today numbering 531 million, spread

over an area of 3,276,141 square kilometres, comprising a bewilder-
ing multiplicity of races, ethnic groups, sub-cultures and religious
sects' (Vatsyayan 1972: 9).

Culture has also been used by the state to govern its subjects.
In colonial times, the government tried to change the meaning of
culture in Indian society by transforming culture into a means as
well as a subject of governance. There were various attempts to collect, document, survey, count, and analyse the cultures of various
communities, to govern them, their collective psyche and identities. Here, culture came into the orbit of state governance (Crook
1968; Grierson 1975). Cultures were targeted 'to know' how to rule
their colonized *praja*. The methods and strategies developed during
colonial governance of culture were to collect, document, and study
which was rare or *anuplabdh* ([unavailable] for colonial sahibs),
amazing, and influential. The line of politics that emerged through
folklore collection and cultural surveys by colonial sahibs was based
on documenting, studying, and representing 'the unique', 'the useful', and 'influential' (Narayan 2001: 55). Thus they paid attention
only to the cultures of communities that appeared unique for the
colonial masters, that seemed useful to understand the societies that
were the target of their total governance, and those related with the
communities that were powerful, dominant, and visible. By visible
they meant socially and economically powerful communities that
supported the colonial government and thereby gave it legitimacy,
and also those subaltern communities that emerged as unlawful,
militant communities requiring authoritative colonial governance.

In post-colonial India a similar line of cultural governance was
continued by the Indian state. Soon after Independence, the indus-
trial- and rural-development model of the economy was cast in the
Five-Year Plan mould. In the First Five-Year Plan (1950–5) the importance of village and small-scale industries was recognized as a means
of employment. Handsome financial provisions were made for their

development within the budget of the central government's Ministry of Commerce and Industries. Ever since, the handicrafts component (inclusive of folk arts) has stayed within the purview of commerce, and has gone through the regular drill of economic development by mass reproduction/marketing through middlemen, modern designer inputs and export. In the initial stages of the Five-Year Plan, it was understood that a ready market existed among foreigners. Emporia and international trade fairs were conceived of as suitable platforms to promote the art-craft-culture industry (Jain 2000: 63). It was in the 1980s, when culture was perceived as a nation-making project that the state planned to use culture with the objective of unifying the nation, creating the Zonal Cultural Centres to reconstitute the national culture and to provide a new space for hitherto invisible popular art forms.

However, despite the well-meaning intentions of the government, the invisibility of marginalized dalit castes in India, especially in UP, can be seen in the attitude of the state towards their culture, and the state-led cultural policies of India, which include funding, have led to suppression of the culture of dalit castes as a whole. For marginalized communities like the dalits and lower castes, the desire to acquire power is strongly linked with the desire to gain representation in history, culture, and public space. This process can be observed in UP where, besides seeking to enhance their political power, the dalits of this state are also trying to gain representation in the historical and cultural spheres and make themselves visible in public spaces. The fulfilment of their desire to gain representation in history can be seen in the surge in the production of numerous dalit popular booklets since the 1960s that highlight the contribution of dalits in India's history. The desire for visibility in public space in towns, cities, and districts is being fulfilled by installing statues of Dalit heroes and constructing parks in their name, while their representation in the cultural field is seen in the revival of their traditional folk songs and dances. Interestingly, the Dalit communities of UP had rejected their cultural traditions between 1950 and 1980 as they developed a new feeling of self-respect, causing them to perceive these cultural forms as symbols of their humiliation. In the last century, the Chamars of UP had also undertaken a social movement to discontinue their caste-based professions of skinning and tanning dead cattle and cutting the umbilical cord of newborn babies. They had also stopped performing their traditional dance called Chamarachna because spectators from the upper and middle castes used to taunt them for these dances. At that time these cultural forms had become a cultural space where they repeatedly faced humiliation from the upper castes.

Today the people of the Chamar community living in various parts of the state are once again keen on reviving these cultural forms as symbols of their self-respect and caste identity in order to acquire representation in public culture as well. For example, the Chamar residents of village Kajishahpur, Khutahan, in Jaunpur district in north India, are eager to revive their folk dance, *Chamaraundha*, which they had rejected many years ago, and for this they are trying to enlist the help of the government. Dalit intellectuals of Allahabad such as Guru Prasad Madan feel that the government should form a cultural policy through which the caste-based culture of the Dalits is revived, while the Dalit cultural association of Azamgarh is constantly demanding that Dalit cultural forms be given importance in the cultural policies of the government. However, if one studies the history of the agenda of the government's cultural policies, one finds that there is minimal space for the culture of the Dalits.

This situation existing in north India is the exact opposite of the one in south India where the backward castes' assertion in states like Tamil Nadu, Karnataka, and Maharashtra started much earlier than in north India. The assertion of the backward castes began in the 1920s and 1930s under the Non-Brahmin Movement or the Self-Respect Movement led by E.V. Ramaswami Naickar, popularly known as Periyar. Periyar's legacy was carried forward by C.M. Annadurai and M. Karunanidhi and several of his followers and aimed to demolish the Brahmins' domination in culture and public institutions. It attacked cultural symbols identified with Hinduism or Brahminism. Periyar preached that the Brahmins had monopolized and cheated other communities for decades and deprived them of self-respect. He stated that most Brahmins claimed to belong to a 'superior' community with the reserved privilege of being in charge of temples and performing *archana*s (prayers). He felt that they were trying to reassert their control over religion by using their superior caste status to claim the exclusive privilege to touch idols or enter the sanctum sanctorum.

The aspirations and ideology of the backward classes were given voice through political parties like the Justice Party, the DMK (Dravida Munnetra Kazhagam), ADMK (Anna Dravida Munnetra Kazhagam), and AIDMK (All India Anna Dravida Munnetra Kazhagam), in addition to a large number of smaller parties of the backward classes in south India. The Dravidar Kazhagam (DK), which was the precursor of the DMK, was the first in post-Independence India to begin a major agitation for backward caste reservations in the erstwhile Madras province in 1950. The backward caste assertion in south India has included all sections of the backward classes like the intermediary castes and the artisanal and service castes. The backward classes are divided among different political parties that seek to espouse backward class causes. They dominate in the politics and economy of the south Indian states and their assertion has eroded the influence of the high castes, which can also be seen in the popular culture of south India.

Two important castes among the Untouchables or Dalits in south India are the Malas and Madigas. The Malas are still very poor labourers but many have taken to education and have joined the middle class. The number of educated professional people with a

Mala background, like doctors, engineers is rising steadily. Many are in government service. Veteran Mala politicians are obviously quite rich. There even are some Mala industrialists. Madigas, one of the largest Scheduled groups in India, have a very ancient presence. They are today mainly poor leather workers and agricultural labourers, although there are references in ancient literature, and stories, which allude to their important role. Both these castes have their own caste-based cultural forms. The Madigas have the *Chindu*, or sword dance, which was prohibited in 1859 and 1874. The dance was performed at festivals, held annually or triennially, in honour of the village goddess, and during the time of threshing corn, building a new house, or the inaugural of a newly dug well. The dance, accompanied by songs containing invective against the Malas, was also performed, under the excitement of strong drinks, in the presence of the goddess, on the occasion of marriages. One verse ran as follows, 'I shall cut with my saw the Malas of the four houses at Nandyal, and, having caused them to be cut up, shall remove their skins, and fix them to drums' (Thurston and Rangachari 1909). The Madigas too contributed a lot to music and dance. The origin for the Jazz drums comes from the primitive but exact rhythm and beat is produced by 'Tappet' or tanned skins covered on round wooden frames. They were played by beating them with two sticks. Sound variation was brought by warming them when the weather was wet and humid.

In UP most of the dalit castes like the Sapera, Nat, Dom, Musahar, Pattharkat, Kanjar, and so on have their own cultural forms, which few people working in the field of culture are aware of. For example, the Doms have their dance called Dom Kuch, the Nats have their Nat Nachna, while communities like the Musahars and Mahavats have their own linguistic register and own song-and-dance tradition through which they express their life struggles, while the Saperas also have their own song-and-dance tradition. Among the Gorh caste there is a popular cultural form called *Huruk Nach*. In this form, the males dress as women and dance to the tunes of the musical instrument called *Huruk*. This a dance-drama form in which there is an anchor or sutradhar known as Harbola who narrates the story. The Huruk Nach is highly popular in villages of UP. In Rajasthan, the culture of the Kalbeliya caste, which is a 'low caste', has been given space in the folk culture of the state and of the country, but the culture of the 'low', marginalized dalit castes of UP have yet to obtain space in the folk culture of the state, let alone of the country as a whole. In this work we will show how the culture of the dalits, especially of the invisible dalit castes, has remained suppressed under government policies that deny them their cultural citizenship, in addition to social and political citizenship.

Organization of the Book

The present book focuses on dalit castes that are voiceless, invisible, and have been left out in the almost 60-year discourse of state-led Indian democracy. It presents a catalogue of the dalits of the dalits, that is of the most marginalized among them who were left out from the discourse of democracy even during the chief ministership of leader of the BSP Mayawati, who claims to work for the uplift of the oppressed and the marginalized (*dabe-kuchle log*) through democratic power. This book focuses on the process of ongoing inclusion of dalits in the democratic sphere and will try to understand the dialectics of contradiction involved in the democratic processes in post-colonial India. It will document, on the one hand, democracy that includes the assertive castes on the margins of politics and governance, while on the other hand excluding many non-assertive and small castes existing on the margins among the margin, as a byproduct of its functional character. It discusses how during the process of democ-ratization of dalit communities some groups are over-represented, while a large number of other castes are still far from the threshold of democracy. These invisible communities among dalits are not even able to demonstrate their politics of presence in the ever-evolving democracy of UP. We will also investigate here the elements and factors that constitute visibility of the marginalized in democratic politics.

There are two ways of looking at democracy. One is the view of the state, policymakers, and so on or the view from the top, which shows the dissemination and spread of democracy. The other view is the one from the bottom. This view helps us understand and grapple with the reality of the spread of democracy, and enables us to observe the groups and communities left out in the process of democratic empowerment. Both these views should be taken together for a fuller and more complete picture of the social matrix.

It is very difficult to tell the stories of such invisibilities and marginalities in one homogeneous narrative form and that is why I will try to tell these stories in different narrative forms. One of the narrative methods that I have used in this book is to begin with the story of a person through whom I have tried to reflect on the whole contemporary history of his/her community. That is why one may find this book a narrative catalogue of human faces of the invisible communities that provides the opportunity to study the various homogeneous categories created by the state and the hierarchical social system. To expand the horizon of those left out and marginalized, I have specially tried to understand the cases of dalit women and tried to document the disconnect between the language and *bhav* (feeling) of dalit rural people and the politics of empowerment of both the state and of the political parties. The book has developed through long-term participant observations of a large number of dalit communities in villages in UP and Bihar and has weaved stories based on interviews, field diaries, case diaries, court judgements, newspaper reports, administrative accounts, folklore—including *lokokti* (folk proverbs), and so on. It also aims to look into the various aspects of stories of exclusion in the dalit community by examining texts, novels, dalit magazines, and other literary sources.

The book is divided into the following chapters. In the Introduction we have prepared the ground for the narrative of investigation of the working of democracy in north India, especially in the context of dalit empowerment in UP, and have tried to discuss invisibility and voicelessness in the context of democracy.

Chapter 1, 'A Beggar's Song of Democracy', focuses on the process of ongoing inclusion of dalits in the democratic sphere of India and tries to understand the dialectics of contradiction involved in the democratic processes in post-colonial India. Indian democracy has included the assertive castes on the margins in the sphere of politics and governance and excluded many non-assertive, small, insignificant lesser dalits as a byproduct of its functional character. The chapter discusses how during the process of democratization of dalit communities some groups are overrepresented, while nearly 62 castes are still far from the threshold of democracy. These invisible and unseen communities amongst the dalits are unable to demonstrate their politics of presence in the ever-evolving democracy of UP. It also investigates the elements and factors that constitute visibility of the marginalized in democratic politics.

Chapter 2, 'Is It a Snake or a Rope? Democracy and Identity Politics in India', documents the changing indicators of visibility in democratic society such as number, caste leaders, and the political representation of caste. There has been a major paradigm shift in the understanding of constituents that make humans important in society. This chapter conducts a critical appreciation of identity politics in north Indian society through a combination of philosophical resources by non-Brahmin sects like Nath Panth and Buddhism and chalks out an ethnography of visibility profile of marginal communities amongst the dalits. It delves into issues of caste identity such as its formation, assertion, and creation of layers of dominance, exclusion, and marginalization. All these aspects present a complex scenario in which the ever-changing flux in the socio-political matrix of democracy is a challenge.

Chapter 3, 'Democracy, Deprivation, and Dispossession: Multiple Narratives of Democracy in North India', documents the multiple experience of democracy in north Indian society through the narratives of small dalit groups in eastern UP. These discourses of multiple marginalizations are crucial to understand how, in the project of empowering communities through state resources and their distribution through state policies, their implementation produces the sense of marginalization among various sections of society.

Chapter 4, 'Margins and Politics: Narratives of Marginalized Dalit Castes', documents how some castes on the dalit margins such as Kasai (butchers), Sapera (snake charmers), Bharbhuja, and so on, imagine their nation by imagining what they aspire to. We have also tried to document the differences in the imagining, representation, and aspirations between developed, educated, and numerically and political visible communities, and those caste and communities that are still invisible and less represented in the universe of democracy. The study is based on narratives collected in two villages in Allahabad district, UP.

Chapter 5, 'With History and Without History: Dalit Reinvention of the Past', focuses on how the history of the communities works as an important constituent in the making of the language of democratic empowerment which helps communities demarginalize themselves. It appears as an important tool for empowerment and progress in the politics of democracy. Both the elite and the assertive margins look towards history for their development and progress. They sense that the dominant ideology of the state and their own privileged access to the state apparatus are both sanctioned by the idea of history (Nandy 2003: 84). The margins and subalterns, on the other hand, contest mainstream history but in the process consciously or unconsciously imbibe some of the mainstream historical ideology. One of the constituents of these historical constructions is the central presence of the state in both the historical narratives—in the elites and the margins. This chapter describes how histories appear in developing demarginalization of the margins and work as a tool for gaining a fair share in the state-led development project. But in this process some of them also form dominant hegemonic and homogenizing sections within the margin itself.

Chapter 6, 'Culture and Representation: The Making of Public Culture', describes how the culture of the dalits is marginalized in the formation of policies around public culture by the state, and even if a few performing arts of the dalits are included, the art forms of the marginalized of the marginalized are totally excluded from the domain of mainstream public culture.

The last chapter presents the conclusions of the study.

Notes

1. Interviewed by Brijendra Gautam in Village Dallipur, Sewapuri Block, district Varanasi on 4 March 2013.
2. Derrida says a similar thing when he points out that when the second person does emerge in inner language it is a fiction; and after all fiction is only fiction (Derrida 1973: 70).
3. 'Pakaha's Wait for Independent India's Constitution', by V.B Rawat. Human Rights. 20 June 2012. See http://blogs.halabol.com/2012/06/20/pakaha%E2%80%99s-wait-independent-india%E2%80%99s-constitution.
4. 'Dalit Women Humiliated and Victimized in Allahahad', by Vidyabhushan Rawat, dated 9 July 2010. See www.countercurrents.org/rawat090710.htm.
5. The meaning of terms and concepts like state and democracy is likely to vary between intellectuals and common people, and also between literates and illiterate, underprivileged populations of various kinds (Kaviraj 2005: 2).

6. A similar observation was made by Dirks who says that during the Mandal crisis caste leaked simultaneously out of the traditional worlds of the subaltern and the village and into the middle-class enclaves of new India. Through the design of the new constitution, the Nehruvian state undertook an immense project of social reform, using the state as the primary instrument to tear down the thousand-year indignities of the caste system (Kaviraj 2005: 13).

7. The state linked various categories in the Indian Constitution to distribute social welfare to the downtrodden communities: these categories are the Scheduled Castes (SCs), Scheduled Tribes (STs) and the Other Backward Classes (OBCs). Currently in UP the SC categories are 64 in number, the ST are 15, and the Backward Class 234. The SCs and the OBCs are scattered in various districts of UP; STs can be found in eastern UP. See http://scholarship.up.nic.in/index.asp.

8. 'SP Takes on Maya, Proposes Dalit Status for 17 OBCs', *Milleniumpost*, 2 April 2013, Lucknow, Team MP.

9. 'SP Takes on Maya, Proposes Dalit Status for 17 OBCs', *Milleniumpost*, 2 April 2013, Lucknow, Team MP.

1

A Beggar's Song of Democracy*

Na kahavaiya ke dosh, na sunvaiya ke dosh, je kahni uparje okar dosh

(It is neither the fault of the teller nor of the listener. It is the fault of the person who has composed the narrative)

This chapter documents how the democratic process of the country includes the assertive margins in the sphere of politics and governance and excludes many of the small, marginalized dalit castes as a byproduct of its functional character. It discusses how during the process of democratization of dalit communities some groups are overrepresented, while many others are still far from the threshold of democracy. These invisible and unseen communities amongst the dalits are unable to demonstrate their politics of presence in the ever-evolving democracy of UP. The chapter is an attempt to understand the dialectics of contradiction involved in the democratic processes in post-colonial India. It also investigates the elements and factors that constitute visibility of the marginalized in democratic politics.

* This chapter has been published as 'A Beggar's Song of Democracy: A Study of Invisible Dalits' in *Handbook of Politics in Indian States: Regions, Parties and Economic Reforms*, edited by Sudha Pai (Oxford University Press, 2013; pp. 269–80).

In a village, 25 kilometres from Allahabad in UP a beggar belonging to the Jogi community of UP, whose traditional occupation is begging, sings this song while seeking alms:

Maiya ke Ram-Ram[1]
Behniya ke Ram-Ram
Bhaiya-Babu[2] *ke Ram-Ram*
Hamra bhi Dhiyaan rakhiyan
Chireya ke Ram-Ram
Churugan[3] *ke Ram-Ram*
Pedh ke Ram-Ram
Pathiai ke Ram-Ram
Hamke na bisriyon

(Salutation to mothers
Salutation to sisters
Salutation to brothers
Look after me too
Salutation to birds
Salutation to tiny birds
Salutation to trees
Salutation to leaves
Forget me not!)

It is ironical that while a dalit woman is leading the BSP, the dalit dominant political party in India, and who has been chief minister of UP several times, a dalit of the same state sings this song. Through the song he tries to remind the people that while some dalit communities are in the centre of dalit discourse and have been included in the democratic processes of the country, many others have remained invisible and marginalized. While the state-led democracy has helped empower many erstwhile marginalized communities, it has also led to the disempowerment of many other small communities. The communities that have gained power do not want to share it with their less fortunate brethren, thus creating a dominant section among the dalits. For example, the Chamar, once a highly marginalized dalit caste in UP, is now one of the most politically powerful, while other castes like Dom, Nat, Sapera, Musahar, and so on, are still not a part of the state and national democratic process.

As we have noted in the introduction, there are two ways of looking at democracy. One is that of the state, policymakers, and so on, wherein a top-down view shows the dissemination and spread of democracy. However, the obverse side of the coin is to view democracy from the bottom, which helps us understand and grapple with the reality of the spread of democracy, making it amply clear who have been left out in this process of democratic empowerment. Both these views should be taken together for a fuller and more complete picture of the social matrix. Here we examine 'how' and 'why' in UP the process of democracy reached a small, select group amongst the dalits, while several others did not even get the briefest glimpse of democratic empowerment. It elucidates the reasons for the political empowerment of the Chamars, which is not only dependent on their large numbers but also on various other significant factors. Besides oral sources, the chapter also aims to look into the various aspects of exclusion in the dalit community by examining texts, novels, and newspaper reports.

Modernity and Shifts in Marginality

Many of the invisible castes of today were earlier categorized as Criminal Tribes under the Criminal Tribes Act passed in 1871 by the Governor-General of India which was amended in 1897. It was first enforced in the northern part of India and later was extended to Bengal (1876) and other areas, with Madras Presidency being the last to enact it in 1911. Under the Act, 150 notified castes of 'hereditary criminals' within the Hindu system were to be kept under police surveillance. More castes were added to the list. The branding of these communities as 'criminal' was not based on the notion of heredity but rather as a community profession passed on from one generation to the next. The Act, therefore, provided for establishing reformatory schools and settlements for the reclamation of these people. Movements of members of the communities were restricted to specific areas and the Act provided for their arrest without warrant if there was any violation. The crimes covered included counterfeiting of coins and currency, murder, theft, robbery, dacoity, and housebreaking. Children in the age-group of 6 to 18 were separated from their parents and put in reformatory schools. In due course Indian society mutely witnessed the emergence of a new class of people who were branded as born criminals. In 1924 the colonial government passed another act for notification, registration, restriction of movements, settlements and schools for criminal tribes, and for sentences. The act made a provision for separate schools for proper education for children of criminal tribes (see Barkan 2000).

These erstwhile criminal tribes were denotified soon after Independence by the Government of India under the Criminal Tribes Act (CTA) of 1952. However, this notification was followed by the substitution of a series of Acts, of which the Habitual Offenders Act (HOA) was the prime one. The HOA preserved most of the provisions of the former CTA, except the premise implicit in it that an entire community can be 'born' criminal. The denotification and the passing of the HOA should have ended the misery of the CTA communities, but it never happened. The police, as well as the people in general, continued with the attitude of looking upon the 'Criminal Tribes' (CTs) as born criminals. The result is that every time there is a petty theft in a locality, the erstwhile CTs are the first suspects. These criminal tribes of yesteryear are today a new social category generally known as the Denotified and Nomadic Tribes of India (DNTs), covering a population approximately of 60 million. Some of them are included in the list of SCs, some in STs, and quite a few in the different formats of BCs. However, many of these tribes do not find a place in any of them. What is common to all these DNTs is the fate of being branded as 'born' criminals.

The story of the DNTs goes back to the early years of colonial rule. In those times, whoever opposed the British colonial expansion was perceived as a potential criminal—particularly if any attempts were made to oppose the government by the use of arms, the charge of criminality was a certainty. Many wandering minstrels, fakirs, petty traders, rustic transporters, and disbanded groups of soldiers were included in the list of criminal groups. Under the colonial notion of projecting itself as the guardian of backward and primitive communities the colonial government tried to show that it had linked these castes with modern education. According to the discourse that originated from colonial knowledge it was tried hard to prove that all these small dalit castes were thieves, criminals, and lazy. This work was first done by colonial administrators and anthropologists, and later by Indian scholars trained under them. The subsequent governments of independent India also tried to prove that they were very concerned about improving their lot (Devy et al. 2013). The famous Indian anthropologist D.N. Majumder has discussed many of these castes in the chapter on Criminal Tribes (Majumder 1941: 188).

During the entire colonial period there was a dilemma on how these small dalit castes should be viewed. An idea about the colonial perspective can be understood a little from the 1931 Census report in which there is a section at the end on Exterior Castes or alienated castes. In this section it was written that the alienated castes of India were self-reliant and could not be called poor from any angle. This category included castes whom Majumder had classified as criminal. It also includes castes like Gareriya (shepherd), Darzi (tailor), and Kori (weavers) that had a good economic condition in the premodern period. Gareriyas made blankets from sheep wool, Koris wove cloth, while Darzis turned it into clothes. These small, now marginalized dalit castes that once had enjoyed a good position in society because of their caste-based skills started losing their source of livelihood, first when the colonial government cut off the source of their livelihood and, second, when it labelled them criminal and lazy (Dwivedi 2008).

When these castes were brought under the Criminal Tribes Act a sense of alienation developed within them as they were viewed with suspicion by the other castes in society. They thus became economic, political, cultural, and social outcastes which caused great harm to them and prevented them from becoming part of the mainstream. However, colonial documents and academic studies have also continually emphasized that these castes were closely linked with the self-reliant village community existing in India from time immemorial. One such caste in this category is the Bansphor whose members are mostly bamboo workers. In the pre-modern society, though untouchable, the Bansphor were a visible community. In the Hindu ritual space, bamboo articles and goods, like the winnow (*soop*), basket (*dalia*), and so on, were used in weddings, for worship, and for festivities and various rituals. This gave the members of the caste social acceptability and they shared an interactive space with the dominant communities. This caste is considered a subcaste of the Dom community and is also known as Bansor, Basar, Dumar, Bansodi, Baskar, and Burud. The name Bansphor is thought to be derived from the Hindi word *bans*, meaning 'bamboo', and *phorna*, meaning 'to split'. The 1981 census of UP reveals that the population of the Bansphor is 18,530 and that in this state, they are largely distributed in Azamgarh, Gorakhpur, Varanasi, Ghazipur, Balia, and Allahabad districts (Prasad 2007: 39).

The social status of the Bansphors declined gradually through the colonial and postcolonial period as the demand for their goods decreased. Since they did not take advantage of modern education and did not search for alternative sources of livelihood they became more and more mired in poverty and illiteracy. Because they were very small in number and could not make up a vote bank for any party, they were not given attention by any political party for political and social mobilization. Furthermore, in the absence of organic intellectuals and conscious and aware members in their caste there was no one to write their caste history and arouse their caste identity through their heroes and history. The Bansphors are honest and hard-working and even today they continue their traditional occupation of weaving baskets and making other bamboo products like winnowing fans, mats, sieves, flutes, and rattles, which they sell at local markets and fairs at very cheap prices. Some keep cattle and pigs, and are drumbeaters for the village. However, they are leading a very pitiable life and survival is not easy for them. It is very difficult for them to acquire bamboo now and they are compelled to buy it at high rates in the urban areas since this is the only means by which they can earn their livelihood. It is very regretful that the middle sections of our society, instead of buying bamboo items from these skilled people, prefer to buy designer bamboo items from modern outlets. This lack of marketing skills is causing this marginalized community to be pushed to the periphery. Furthermore, at present, the community has not adapted to changing times. Instead, they are still stuck with traditional work. The high cost of bamboo has hurt its vocation sharply despite the fact that bamboo products are associated with craft and utility items of daily use. 'In 1950–60, the cost of a bamboo was merely three or four rupees but now, a 25-foot long bamboo costs Rs 170,' says Kailashnath,[4] who lives in the squatter (temporary slum) colony near Minto Park, Kydganj, Bhargava Road, Allahabad. Another youth of this community, Manoj who lives in the same colony, said, 'It's like digging a well anew every day to drink water. When we go to buy a bamboo, we can't buy as it is expensive, and when we wish to sell the bamboo products, we have to sell at very low rates that don't cover the cost of the bamboo, as no one is willing to buy at higher prices.'[5]

Vibrant 50-year-old Sushila still takes pride in the community's traditional vocation, and sings a song celebrating the importance of bamboo, which represents the collective consciousness of the Bansphor community.[6] The song is given below:

Bans kayi khatiya
Bans kayi jhapli
Bans kayi udankhatola ho
Na chahi haman ko mahal dumahala
Na chahi peeth patola ho
Jodat jadat tan jari jaihai
Banchahi tikhati bans re.

(A bamboo cot
A bamboo basket
An aircraft of bamboo be,
I need no castle, nor palace
Not a yellow robe for me,
Fighting and struggling, body decays
Yet bamboo stays for you and me.)

Another similar invisible and marginalized dalit caste of UP is the Baheliya. They are a community of hunters and birdcatchers and their name originates from the Sanskrit *vyadka*, meaning 'one who pierces'. In addition they also extract honey from beehives and gather peacock feathers to make fans. The Baheliyas are distributed in the central and western parts of UP and, according to the 1981 Census, their population is 57,470. They are divided into six groups—the Aheria, Gehlot, Sissodia, Karaul, Pasi, and the Muslim Baheliya. Since catching birds is now banned, they augment their economic resources by selling vegetables, pulling rickshaws, cutting wooden planks, and making hog hair brushes (Bharti 1997: 137). The Baheliyas were not so important in the ritual system of the upper castes but they were not untouchables and because they were nomadic and wandered in the forests catching birds they were not oppressed so much by the upper castes under the Brahminical system. They had indigenous knowledge of trees, birds, and wildlife and so they enjoyed prestige among the other communities living in and around the forests and thus were also quite visible. However, now that all the forests have been acquired by the State they have less space to wander freely in them. Also, because of their fewer number they cannot pressure the State to provide them space either in forest-based or in urban development.

Apart from the Bansphor and Baheliyas, two other small and invisible castes found in rural UP are the Nat and Mahavat, whose traditional occupation was rearing cattle. As the market economy took the villages in its grip these castes suffered great loss as organizations like Belgian American Education Foundation (BAEF) entered the field of animal husbandry and took it over. The people of these castes earlier kept stud buffaloes whose services were sought for impregnating she-buffaloes. They managed to earn quite a bit between August and October and that would see them through the year. They also had good knowledge of the common illnesses of cattle and were much sought after, as they were relevant to the village economy. Nats were also professional acrobats and gymnasts and before the advent of gymnasiums and muscle-building medicine, they trained village youths in wrestling. However, they have now been replaced by private trainers and have been edged out of their livelihoods. They often ply rickshaws or work as labourers on construction sites.

Homogeneity, Multiple Layers, and Hierarchy

As mentioned in the 'Introduction', the Chamar caste, which is numerically the largest dalit community of UP, has emerged as the most dominant one and has cornered all the benefits of the process of dalit empowerment while many of the numerically smaller communities are still marginalized from the democratic processes of both the dalits and of the nation as a whole. A similar situation was observed in Maharashtra where the Mahars (Ambedkar's caste), which is largest in number, started becoming the dominant group although Ambedkar tried to mobilize the dalits as a homogeneous group. In this process, the Matang and other smaller dalit communities became marginalized. Though Ambedkar vehemently denied that he discriminated against the Matangs, differences emerged within the dalit community resulting in the practice of exclusion.

In UP too there exists exclusion within the dalit castes which was strengthened rather than eradicated in the process of democratic mobilization. Kanshiram, who belonged to the Chamar caste, while founding the BSP in the state, said, 'The state between Ganga and Yamuna, Uttar Pradesh is *Aryavrath* (Brahmin-dominated). I will transform it into *Chamarvrath* (Chamar-dominant).' He rallied the Chamars from Punjab to Bihar who, he said, would form the base of the BSP as he believed that in the country if there was any community after the Brahmins who were the most educated it was the Chamars (Akela 2007: 20). He thus opined that the nucleus of the BSP from Punjab to Bihar would be the Chamars while the other dalit communities would also be linked with the BSP. He broke the dependence of this large and politically potent social group on other political parties led by the leaders of the forward and backward castes. It is worth mentioning that Mayawati, whom he nominated to take his place as leader of the BSP, also belongs to the Chamar caste. The Chamar dominance in BSP has excluded several dalit communities who are still languishing in the margins of the margin. Recently, out of the 200 SC candidates recruited in Noida Authority, 199 belonged to the Chamar caste. One of the speakers dissented saying that the BSP seems to have forgotten that all dalit castes had unified to ensure BSP's victory in 2007.[7]

Like the Chamars, two other dalit castes, namely Pasi and Dhobi, have also made their places in government jobs, business, and agriculture. The Pasi, basically a warrior caste, have many members working as high-level officers and politicians. The Dhobis, whose profession was washing clothes, are also engaged in agriculture, animal husbandry, and other agricultural activities. These castes have associated themselves with education, are active in democratic politics and have their own community leaders. They also possess written history and caste legends about their origins and through them they express their desire of assertion. They also have popular booklets written by people of their own community narrating their suffering, oppression, and humiliation in the past by upper castes in spite of their crucial role in the making of the nation and the society. They use these narratives of sufferings in the past to demand state support for their mobility.

The Making of the Chamars

The Chamars became developed and a part of the Indian nation through their capacity to desire. The capacity to desire[8] connotes a condition in which a community acquires at least a minimum level of material development and societal recognition from where they might articulate their latent dreams and desires for a better life and speak about it to others with pride. This would make them vocal and dominant in a way that others take notice of them and respect their aspirations. These are achieved through different ways of assertion like forming caste and group alliances that place them visibly in the democratic sphere and, in turn, give them a better leverage to negotiate. They acquire the language, idioms, diction, images, metaphors, and mediums to interact with the state that it understands, that is, the lingua franca of governance (Appadurai 2004: 59–84). The capacity of the Chamars to desire helped the modern dalit think tank and leader, Kanshiram, to translate this politics of presence into the politics of representation.

The Chamars were traditionally involved in skinning dead animals, tanning leather, and manufacturing leather goods while their women-folk cut umbilical cords of newborn babies of upper-caste households. Being an untouchable caste, the Chamars were oppressed in their rural life and this led them to migrate to big cities to better their economic conditions during the colonial period. They chose various occupations like grass-cutting, musical performance, and so on. During the mid-eighteenth century Chamars were recruited as menials and domestics by the Europeans in towns and cities. Tracing the caste ethnography of Chamars in the early twentieth century, Briggs establishes how even at that time they had become a well-established community (Briggs 1920: 22). Some of them turned vegetarian to free themselves of the stigma of untouchability. Two prominent sub-castes of the Chamars, namely Jatiya and Jaiswar predominate in UP. Both these sub-castes claim higher social status in the caste hierarchy and many amongst the Jatiya are well-to-do. The Jaiswars' claim to superiority was based on their refusal to do degrading jobs and their efforts to better their economic condition. Some Jaiswars were with the troops that fought with Clive's forces at Plassey (Briggs 1920: 23). The Jatiyas too had freed themselves from degrading jobs in west and central UP in the early twentieth century. From the late nineteenth century, untouch-able caste groups, particularly the Chamars, migrated from rural areas to Allahabad, Varanasi, Kanpur, and Lucknow, to perform menial services. The British military and civil administration which was con-solidated in towns after the 1857 Mutiny also employed Chamars as domestic servants and retainers as these jobs were not performed by caste Hindus. In Kanpur, Chamars were employed in leather facto-ries and tanneries set up by the government and British industrialists (Gooptu 2006: 4–5).

Being close to the Europeans in the eighteenth century some dalits, especially Chamars, came in contact with the western influ-ences. They acquired a working knowledge of English and other

European languages and also acquired education through mission schools. In the armed forces too education had been made free and compulsory for boys and girls and if the guardians did not send their children to school they were penalized. Education opened their minds and widened their horizons and a Chamar intelligentsia emerged from amongst them (Bechain 1997: 177). During the colonial period many caste associations were formed in north India such as the Bharat Sat Samaj, Bharatiya Dusadh Samaj, Bihar Rajak Sangh, Jatavbir Mahasabha, Jaat-Paat Torak Mandal, Musahar Sewak Sangh, and so on, which began the mission of spreading education and reforming society. They inspired the dalits to link themselves with the education system (Choudhary and Shrikant 2005). When Mahatma Gandhi launched the campaign of uplifting untouchables through Harijan Sevashrams, many dalit workers received education and associated themselves with the Gandhian concept of nationalism. Alongside, Hindu nationalists like Madan Mohan Malviya also helped in educating the dalits in their own ways. The educational institutions set up by the Arya Samaj played an important role, particularly in western UP, in educating the Jatavs, a sub-caste of the Chamars (Lynch 1974: 67–8).

The making of the Chamar intelligentsia began with the emergence of the middle class which was triggered by the spread of education in the 1920s. Five important elements led to the emergence of a Chamar middle class. First, there was exposure to other influences because of migration from rural to urban areas. Second, they gave up lowly jobs traditionally assigned by the Brahminical system that tarnished their caste identities. Third, the dissemination of education was another important landmark. Fourth, there was the emergence and development of community leaders charged with the zeal of modernity and democratic values. Finally, identity assertion got a boost through various symbolic means like caste histories, and heroes in the form of chapbooks (popular booklets). These factors led to the emergence of the middle class, which had acquired the capacity to aspire, resulting in the germination of the politics of democratic participation. The educated Chamars created a niche for themselves in society whereas other marginalized castes could not do so. Although dalit intellectuals also emerged from castes like the Khatik, Bhangi, Pasi, and Dhobi, and other such lower castes in the Allahabad region during the colonial period but the number of intellectuals from the Chamar community outnumbered them. Some of these non-Chamar intellectuals were Khemchand Bohare (1875–1960) from Agra; Choudhary Mulkiram (1910–1954) from Hapur; Choudhari Nandlal (1862–1943) from Allahabad; Dharam Prakash (1900–1972) from Bareli; Manikchand Jatavaveer (1897–1956) from Agra; Karan Singh Kaen (1898–1990); Puranchand (1900–1970); Sundarlal Sagar (1896–1952); Pyarelal Kuril (1916–1984) from Ghatampur, Unnao; Gopichandra Pipal (1901–1989) from Kanpur; Sadhu Jitau from Sahijanpur, Lucknow; Swami Achhutananda (1879–1933) from Farukhabad; Swami Prabhutananda Vyas (1877–1950) from Agra; and Ramnarayan Yadavendu (1909–1951) (Kshirsagar 1994: 372). Dr Ambedkar also played an important role in the spread of education among the dalits. For him the solution to all dalit problems lay in education. By positioning education as an important agenda in social reform, he proposed knowledge as a tool to be used for dalit liberation. Many of the Chamars who had migrated to Kolkata and Mumbai were inspired by Ambedkarite thoughts and motivated the people of their native villages to educate their children (Hans 2003: 77). Several Ambedkar libraries and Ambedkar trusts, including the registered Ambedkar Library set up in Allahabad in 1935–6, came up in Dalit colonies across India and many Dalit communities started moving ahead by acquiring education in large numbers.

A study of the oral history of the process of acquiring education and becoming intellectuals by a section of the dominant Dalit group in Allahabad, Kanpur, and Lucknow shows that migration to cities and settling in cantonment areas were important factors in this process. This can be seen as a 'cantonment phenomenon', since the cantonments and the British army officers played a crucial role in educating the dalits who worked in their houses as domestic help. One such dalit intellectual and popular writer, Baudhacharya S. Rao Sajivan Nath, while reminiscing about his days in the cantonment, says, 'We lived in the cantonment area. My father worked in the house of a British army officer. The officer himself got my siblings and I admitted in a school. I must tell you that the British don't have any casteist feelings, which the so-called upper castes have that even the shadow of an Untouchable will pollute them. Since childhood, we saw one family member cleaning the boots of the British officers, while someone else would feed their children. In other words, we lived with them as a part of their family. The language spoken by all of us was a Pidgin English, which was called Garauti English stemming from the word *gora* that was used for the whites. In fact, all the dalits who spoke Garauti English were highly respected by the other Dalits in the dalit colony. People used to say admiringly, "Wow! So-and-so can speak Garauti English!" We learnt Garauti English just as children learn their mother tongues whether they can read and write or not. All of us who knew Garauti English later learnt English as a part of our education, which we all acquired till whatever level possible. Because of the British, the urge for education increased among the Dalits.'

After leaving the cantonment some of the educated, intellectual Chamars started working for the community's liberation. All of them believed that spreading education among the grassroots Dalits was one of the ways to achieve this goal. In our colony lived an intellectual named Rai Sahab Kakarni who ran an Ambedkar library in his house. There were other intellectuals, too, like Bihari Lal and Dr Nandlal Jaiswar, who were extremely knowledgeable. They used to write chapbooks for the Dalits to read. One booklet that was very popular in those days was *Daliton ki Awaaz Babu ke Saamne*. All this shows that even during the British period, a large number of dalit Chamars were educated intellectuals.[9]

During the colonial period several dalit publishing houses were set up by these Chamar intellectuals to publish magazines and newspapers. In the erstwhile United Provinces, the forerunner of Hindi dalit journalism was Swami Achhutananda who launched the newspaper *Achhut* in 1917. In 1924 Santram launched the monthly *Usha*, and *Adi Hindu* of Swami Achhutananda was launched in 1928. On 1 June 1934, Munshi Hariprasad Tamta launched the Hindi weekly, *Samta*. The process continued even after Independence and in 1957 the Hindi weekly, *Singhnaad* was launched by Dayanand Vyas. In 1962, *Zamin ke Taarey* was published from Aligarh, by Mewaram Mahasay, while Balbir Singh Azad published *Soshit Pukar*, a Hindi weekly, from Bulandshahar, in September 1966. The Hindi weekly, *Swadhin Bharat*, launched in 1968, was published from Aligarh. Mohandas Nemisharay from Meerut launched two magazines: a weekly, *Samta Shakti*; and a fortnightly, *Bahujan Adhikar*, in 1972 and 1981, respectively (Bechain 1997: 252–6). In the 1960s many middle class, educated Chamars and other dalits who wanted to spread the notion of dalit empowerment among the grassroots started writing chapbooks (booklets printed on coarse paper). These publications, magazines and chapbooks, helped assert dalit identity, paving the way for their political empowerment through the making of the dalit public. The writers are now spread all over UP and they strive hard to disseminate the message of dalit consciousness through their books.

Emergence of Their Own Politics

In the dalit politics that emerged in UP after Independence the Chamar intellectuals and community leaders were in the forefront since they had acquired the capacity to aspire for democratic participation. In the absence of such leaders in other dalit communities, the Chamars were in a better bargaining capacity to take advantage of democracy and the state. In the 1950s, the Chamars who were still engaged in the polluting caste-based profession launched the Nara Maveshi Movement, which was their attempt to free themselves from the low-caste-based, polluting profession and exercise their fundamental right to choose the profession they desired to engage themselves in. This movement had a significant impact on the Chamars and attaining freedom from menial jobs helped them gain social respectability. They also started developing their own politics when Kanshiram, who was a Ravidasia Chamar from Punjab, entered the scenario of dalit politics. Although Kanshiram developed as a leader of dalits as a whole, a major chunk of the BSP was made up of Chamars since he found that in UP there were pockets of highly aware Chamars who had played an active role in the Nara Maveshi Movement in the 1950s. He thus found a readymade cadre for the party in its initial phase and these activists of the Nara Maveshi Movement were the foot soldiers of the BSP.

The dominance of the Chamar in the politics of UP vis-à-vis other dalit communities may be evidenced by examining the caste-wise analysis of the BSP government in UP. It reveals that out of a total of 52 ministers only eight belong to the dalit caste. Five belong to the Chamar caste, and only one of each belongs to Dusadh, Pasi, and Mallah castes. There is no representation in the BSP ministry from dalit castes like Basor, Dhanuk, Balmiki, Dom, Gond, Kol, Dharikar, Musahar, Beldar, Bhuaiar, Hela, Baiswar, Bansphor, Beriya, Pankha, and so on. In fact, out of 403 MLAs in the UP Assembly, BSP's share of total seats is 206, out of which 100 are BSP dalit MLAs. The share of Chamar seats might at best be approximated, but one may deduce that most of them are from this dominant caste. It is sad that Mayawati's party has neither addressed, nor solved the problems of how to mobilize all or most of the SCs.

Not only in reservation but in government jobs also such differences are visible. According to the 2001 Census report the scheduled castes like Chamar, Dhusiya, and Jatav had 59.67 per cent representation in various government jobs while the representation of OBCs like Ahir, Yadav, Yaduvanshi, and Gwala in government jobs was only 34.49 per cent.[10]

Even the initiative taken by the state government to bring about an amendment in the reservation quota in employment in 2001 could not be implemented. A Social Justice Committee was formed to propose on the reservation policy. It presented in its report that the 66 Scheduled Castes in UP be divided into two groups: amongst them 55.70 per cent population comprising Chamars, Dhusiyas, and Jatavs should be given 10 per cent reservation, and the remaining 44.30 per cent population comprising 63 other castes should be given 11 per cent. This proves that some dominant castes have received more importance in democracy as compared to the other marginalized castes.[11]

The road to Chamar domination amongst the dalits crossed important milestones, namely mobility and migration; spread of education; economic betterment; emergence of community leaders; creation of self-respect through identity assertion, and political representation. Though other dalit communities have had reservations in democratic bodies, government jobs, and educational institutions, the reins of political power have never been in their hands specifically when we talk about the marginalized dalit castes. Every political party pays lip sympathy to the cause of the SCs but the levers of power have invariably been with the Hindu upper castes, dominant middle castes and the Chamars.

A byproduct of the empowerment of the Chamars was that they started excluding those who continued with the traditional caste-based occupations and even amongst the Chamars a caste-based hierarchy was formed. Occupation created barriers and often became a bar to marriage even within the same group. Those who removed manure or night soil could not inter-marry those who served as *Sais*. *Rai Dasis* did not marry Jatiyas who skinned carcasses. Similarly, the Jatiyas who worked with the skins of 'unclean' animals could not marry those who did not. There were instances where the Kurils who tanned did not marry those who made shoes. Thus social hierarchy resulting in exclusion is rampant within the community as well.

Laggards and Left-outs

In sharp contrast to the Chamar is the Bhangi community of UP comprising Helas (40,678; 0.12 per cent) and the Lal Begi (299; percentage very insignificant). Traditionally treated as untouchable, the community was historically restricted to three occupations: cleaning toilets, sweeping, and scavenging (which sometimes involves handling dead bodies). Efforts have been made to improve sanitation systems in India, including laws that ban the construction of dry toilets and the manual removal of human waste but despite this the Bhangis continued to work in their traditional roles and they continued to face severe social barriers and discrimination. However, when they migrated to cities they developed their own deities, created their own religious spaces and followed almost the entire trajectory of the Chamars except that they did not claim their share in the political sphere. Though there were small efforts by this community in colonial times to carve a place for themselves in politics they were too short-lived and petered away. Badri Prasad Balmikinanda was perhaps the first person of this community who followed in the footsteps of Ambedkar to spread the light of education amongst the Balmiki youth. In Allahabad, he established Rishikul Pathshala which has now grown into an intermediate college. He travelled to various cities to inspire the community to lead a clean life, shun dirty work, and send their children to schools (Bharti 1997: 56–7). Balmikinanda made some efforts to develop a different political line for the Balmikis; he joined the Congress and was close to H.N. Bahuguna. However, the community played second fiddle in the political space and was happy to follow rather than lead. This sharp difference with the Chamars cost them their democratic empowerment. Furthermore, unlike the Chamars, the Balmikis did not shun their caste-based occupation thus denying themselves social emancipation. They did not diversify into other trades and occupations and thus free themselves of the stigma of untouchability that is most important for equality, the cornerstone of democratic empowerment.

The problem of lack of visibility in a marginalized community is exemplified by the Bahelias. They have their own informal caste council known as a *biradari panchayat*, which is present in every Bahelia settlement. The panchayat consists of five members elected by members of the community. As a dalit community, the Bahelias often suffer from societal discrimination. The panchayat, which acts as an instrument of social control dealing with issues such as divorce and adultery, has also created vocal community leaders who seek betterment of the community by influencing political parties. On 8 May 1997 a community leader, M.A.A. Fatmi, raised the issue of the ban on catching, hunting, and selling birds in the Parliament and the entire community staged protests against this move (Bharti 1997: 137), showing that the seeds of protest and politics are present in them. However, the unwillingness of the community to break the shackles of traditional occupations has stunted its economic betterment and the capacity to aspire for a better and respectable life. The community might come out of its inertia if its leaders took proactive steps to rehabilitate the community through education and identity assertion and give voice to their political aspirations (Bharti 1997: 138).

For democratic visibility and political empowerment along with migration and mobility, education and aspiration for socio-economic betterment are essential. The Chamars understood this necessity long back, which enabled them to move ahead on the path of political empowerment and socio-economic development. At present some marginalized dalit communities are now surging ahead on the path pioneered by the Chamars and are using their experiences for democratic participation and for raising the self-esteem and self-confidence of the caste. A case in point is the marginalized Jogi community, which is so insignificant that it does not appear amongst the list of 66 SCs in UP. It is an extremely backward dalit community whose caste-based profession is begging. This caste is mainly concentrated in UP districts like Faizabad, Pratapgarh, Jaunpur, Sultanpur, and Varanasi and constitutes nearly 40 per cent of the total Muslim population (Narayan 2006: 60). The Hindus amongst them are *sadhus*, while those who embraced Islam are known as 'Jogi Faqir'. The Jogis consider themselves superior to Brahmins as they claim that Lord Shiva belongs to their community but other communities assign them a low position. Although begging is the caste-based slot of this caste the younger generation has taken up various occupations like running small shops and serving in both government and private sectors. Due to this there is increased migration and mobility among the caste members.

The Jogis remained deprived of all the developmental benefits for a long period of time. The literacy rate of this caste is less than one per cent. They do not have a caste council but they have group organizations comprising the *chelas* (disciples) of the same *guru* (religious master). They generally resolve their differences through the elders of the community as they do not have any village panchayat. If the differences are not resolved they go to the court of law (Singh 2005: 644). Since they did not have caste councils the traditional resources of making community leaders were unavailable to them, which is in sharp contrast to the presence of caste councils and community leaders in dalit communities like Chamar, Pasi, and Dhobi. Neither the government nor the elders of this community were concerned about the plight of these people. When the people of this caste went to government officials to claim some benefits provided to SCs they were turned away saying that Muslims did not fall within the definition of the SCs. But, gradually, Jogis are progressing towards the struggle for recognition and development. In recent times they have had some electoral gains in local bodies and are moving forward on the path of economic empowerment. They too are following the same trajectory of the Chamars to gain dominance. They are also developing their own community leaders who are facilitating their uplift. One such community leader of this caste is Dr Moharram Ali. He took the initiative of linking this caste with the dalit movement led by the BSP. The first thing that he did was to collect the caste history of the Jogis from the older members. He then wrote a booklet narrating its caste glory and disseminated it among the illiterate Jogis to raise their self-esteem. When the other castes heard about the past glory of the Jogis they too felt impressed. This elevated the pride of the Jogis, built up their self-confidence and helped in their identity assertion that was crucial for political mobilization and development. The history of the Jogis reveals that they were earlier a Hindu marginalized lower caste called Gosai. A roving saint (*jogi*) of this caste converted to Islam and the present-day Jogis are his descendants. The Jogi from whom the caste claims its lineage could perform miracles. This made him very popular among the people who gave him alms as reward. His descendants continued to follow this profession which eventually became a caste-based one. Its members claim that although they are Muslim by religion, culturally they are Hindu. Today, the Jogis have acquired the confidence to contest elections for the post of gram pradhan in their villages and some have even won (Bharti 1997: 81–2).

Although developmental programmes have not been launched specifically for the Jogi community, in rural areas a few of them are benefiting from various government developmental programmes.

In the urban areas, however, the Jogis are deprived of benefits from all such programmes. They prefer education for their children but their economic condition does not allow prolonged education for daughters and most drop out after middle school (Singh 2005: 643). The zeal for education has fired the new generation and they now understand that good education translates into good jobs.

For democracy to spread in its sweep, range and depth, it will have to include the hitherto latent and unseen dalit communities like the 62 dalit communities in UP. For this the communities that are on the margin of the margins will have to take the roadmap provided by the major and dominant dalit castes. They need to acquire visibility which is possible only through acquiring the capacity to desire through the means that empowered the other dalit castes, especially the Chamars. These lesser dalit groups need to counter their disembodiment and to do what they need to develop their own politics.

It is the ethical and moral aspect of democracy that it links those who are languishing on the margins of the margin. Democracy, by definition, should reach out to the last man. In fact, it should begin with the last man and move to the major groups, but unfortunately this does not happen. It moves from top to bottom. It is also the moral and ethical responsibility of the dalit movement that it practise inclusion instead of exclusion; it should give importance and credence to the meek and weak voices. The dominant dalit groups who now have control over scarce resources should act as agencies to help distribute them to the poorest of the poor rather than gobble them up themselves. In fact, for dalit politics to be sharp and dynamic it is necessary that all smaller and lesser dalit groups who are now invisible and unseen, are included within its socio-political matrix. The Jogi beggar's song of democracy is a heart-rending cry. He pleads acceptance in the democratic process with his salutations and his agony is sharpened by his deep sense of alienation. He feels left out, excluded, ignored, and he thus begs attention!

In this chapter, we have identified some of the marginalized among the marginalized dalit castes and tried to examine what factors led to the empowerment of some dalit castes and to the disempowerment of some others. In the next chapter we will try to understand who are the people who imagine their nation and how the marginalized of the marginalized castes imagine the nation.

Notes

1. *Ram-Ram*: A popular salutation in the name of the renowned Hindu deity Lord Rama.
2. *Bhaiya-Babu*: Akin to Big Brother; an elderly man of lower social strata addresses a young boy with affectionate respect and adds 'Babu' after 'Bhaiya'.
3. *Churugan*: Tiny birds.
4. Interviewed by Ramashankar Singh, 28 January 2011. See Singh 2015.
5. Interviewed by Ramashankar Singh, 28 January 2011. See Singh 2015.
6. Interviewed by Ramashankar Singh, 28 January 2011. See Singh 2015.
7. *Hindustan* (2011), 'Baspa ne Daliton ki Ekta Todi', *Hindustan*, Allahabad, 25 May, p. 2.
8. We use the term initially used by Appadurai, extending its connotations to suit our findings.
9. Interview with Baudhacharya S. Rao Sajivan Nath, Allahabad, 12 July 2006.
10. 'Jitna Chahiye Usse Adhik Mil Chuka Hai Aarakshan', *Amar Ujala*, 12 September 2013.
11. 'Failon Mein Kaid Hai Aarakshan Mein Sanshodhan', *Hindustan*, 13 September 2013.

2

Is It a Snake or a Rope?

Democracy and Identity Politics in India

'Inequality is the official doctrine of Brahminism.'
—Ambedkar, quoted in Rathore and Verma (2011: 161)

'Margins are as plural and diverse as the centres.'
—Chakrabarty (2007: 16)

Jativad bandhan, gotravad bandhan, maanvad bandhan, aavah-vivah bandhan chodkar, anupam vidya-charan-sampadda pratyaksh ki jati hai.

'Shedding caste bondage, family-and-clan (gotra) tie-ups, matrimonial alliances, the beauteous wealth of knowledge is experienced.'
—Mahatma Buddha in *Ambatth Sutth* (Sankrityayan 1930: 201)

This chapter documents the changing indicators of visibility in democratic society such as numbers, caste leaders, and the political representation of castehood. The pluricultural nature of Indian society has given rise to a great deal of inequality, both horizontal and vertical, in Indian democracy. Horizontal inequality is inequality between groups, which is distinct from vertical inequality, or inequality among individuals (Stewart 2009). Among the dalits, who are homogeneously accorded a subordinate position by the upper castes despite the fact that they comprise a highly heterogeneous population, there exists horizontal inequality, which is not only socio-economic in nature, but also political. Through a case study of the Chamar caste we will show how horizontal marginality exists within this caste that is distinct from vertical marginality with upper castes.

Beneficiaries and Deprived: Formation of the Untouchable of Untouchables

Traditionally, the Chamars were engaged in two activities, both of which were considered dirty, polluting, and demeaning for their caste. The men were involved in skinning and tanning the hides of dead cattle (*maveshi*), while the women used to cut the umbilical cord (*nara*) of women during childbirth, and clean their dirt and pollutants. These two activities were the ones that rendered them untouchable for the other castes, but were also very important in the social system. When the Chamars understood that these two activities were the causes of their untouchability, around the 1950s the Chamars of north India started the Nara-Maveshi Movement (NMM) to shed their demeaning caste-based professions. During the movement, when the Chamars abstained from doing this work, several villages of UP were transformed into 'suppression nodes' for the dalits, particularly the Chamars. The ruling classes in collusion with the police—who were tacitly or openly supporting the *savarna* castes (upper castes)—inflicted suffering on the dalits, despite many laws against untouchability. Some of the laws and provisions enacted against untouchability in the Constitution for the protection of the rights of dalits like the Prevention of Atrocities Act (1989), Anti-Untouchability Offence Act (1955) and Protection of Civil Rights Act (1973), among others empowered the dalits to fight the injustices inflicted on them, such as during the Nara-Maveshi activism, and also lent confidence to their political assertions.

This movement spread through much of the rural areas of Bihar and UP. It reached many villages in almost all parts and regions of UP. The movement is remembered by various names at various places. Other than the 'Nara-Maveshi Movement' it is also called 'Nara-Vyaur' and 'Murda-Maveshi' Movement. The forward and middle castes and non-Chamar dalit castes in the villages, who came together against the Chamars during this movement, remember this episode in rather derogatory-sounding phrases such as 'Chamar andolan' (Chamar movement), 'Chamaro ka utpat' (hooliganism of the Chamars), and so on. After a long battle, the Chamars acquired the right to shift their occupation from *chamra-haddi* (hide/leather and bone) work to other livelihood options. This movement played a significant role in liberating a sizeable part of the Chamar community from untouchability, helped in their progress, educated them and encouraged them to modify their professions. Simultaneously, the movement also played a crucial role in the development of a political dalit public in the rural areas of UP. Many of those associated with the movement are today organizing others around similar issues and a cadre has also emerged that is working as an agency for dissemination of political ideas and awareness that provides a strong base for the BSP.

When the Chamars resident in the villages stopped doing their traditional work, other Chamars were brought in from areas like Rewa and Bilaspur and even from parts of Bihar and were settled in the villages. To this day, these immigrants earn their livelihood by doing the traditional work of cutting the umbilical cord and clearing and cleaning carcasses. They even tolerate the taunt of 'untouchability'. They are referred to as Kor Chamar in these villages and the other castes of the village treat them the same way as they earlier treated the Chamars who had traditionally lived in these villages. They do not have any relations with them nor drink water touched by them. These Kor Chamars continue to be treated as untouchables and have to sit apart in village marriages and ceremonies. In this way, untouchability has not been eradicated in rural society even today as an untouchable section has developed within the erstwhile untouchable caste. This phenomenon can also be observed in village Shahabpur in UP, where a few Chamars were brought in from Madhya Pradesh with their families and settled there to do work no longer done by the Chamars of the village.

Shahabpur village is located 25 kilometres from Allahabad, on the Lucknow highway. It is inhabited by people of various castes, most of them belonging to the lower strata in the caste hierarchy. Castes like the Patels, Pasis, Mauryas, Kumhars, Chamars, Turks (Muslims), and Dhobis, who are greater in number, are mostly settled in their own caste-based *patti*s (small hamlets and subhamlets, also called *poorva*s and *tola*s). Other castes like Yadavs, Darzis, Lohars, Nais, Bhujas, Dafalis, and Churihars, who are fewer in number, live mostly in the Shahabpur Bazaar or are scattered in other pattis. Although Chamars have their own patti in the village called 'Godam' the Chamars who have migrated from Madhya Pradesh are not allowed to settle there. They live in the fringes of Shahabpur Bazaar.

Through the narratives of the Kor Chamars one can understand the class difference that exists within the Chamars at present. Sarju, also called Sarajudin, who along with a few others like him, performs the caste-based activities of the Chamars that have been discarded by the original Chamars of the village like tanning and skinning cattle hides, told us the story of the Kor Chamars of Shahabpur.

'When the Chamars of Shahabpur and the adjoining villages stopped doing the Nara Maveshi (sauriyahi and carcass) work the Thakurs of Shahabpur Akshay Pratap Singh brought us here from Rewa and settled us in the village. This was around 1974–5. When we were settled here the Patels protested against it since they used to bring in Chamars from adjoining villages like Kachhare and Gopiya to do this work and they felt that their men would suffer if we replaced them. Also, the Patels lived just behind our settlement and they felt offended that we were staying in their vicinity. The reason was that the place would get polluted because of our work and also that had the land remained vacant they could have encroached on it. They uprooted our huts and burnt them down and police cases were filed against them. The sarkar (police "darogaji" and DMji "administration") came to our support. It was only gradually that they accepted our presence and we were allowed to settle down in the village'.[1]

'Three families came from Rewa to work here. One was our family, the second was the family of Ram Nihore, and the third was the family of Radheysham. We are all related to each other. We are Chamar by caste. Our surname in Rewa was Saket. Now we use the surname Ravidas. After coming here we started doing *sauriyahi* and carcass work in Shahabpur and adjoining villages. We earn only Rs 800 to 1200 by selling bones, and Rs 100 for the skin of small animals and Rs 200 for the skin of big animals, which is very little. These are bought by Muslim butchers, who come in vans from places like Mauama and Baghigaharpur. They then sell the bones to traders in the Kareli area of Allahabad who make fertilizers from them. The skin is sold to traders in Kanpur for making leather. Our women who cut the cords of newborn children and clean the mothers are given one kilo of rice and old clothes for their work, which also works out to very little. So we supplement our family income by working as field labourers, brickfield labourers, working as cobblers, growing vegetables by taking land on lease, and so on. We have no land and if we did we would not have done the dirty work we are forced to do'.[2]

'The Chamars who have left this work look at us with great disgust. We have no *roti-beti sambandh* (food and marriage interactions) with them. They do not invite us to their gatherings and do not drink water from our hands. They treat us like untouchables. However, during election time they come to us to request us to vote BSP and they also take us with them to cast our votes. We also participate in Ravidasi satsangs with them as we too follow the Ravidasi sect like them'.

'We are living here but we still feel like outsiders. All our relatives and our *kul-devtas* are in Rewa. We go there for marriages and other occasions and also to pray to our kul-devtas. However we have been given the *baasgeet parcha* (notice of permanency) for our place of stay in Shahabpur and we also have BPL and APL cards for obtaining ration and other welfare measures'.

Sarju said that all he wants now is that his children should get education and that they should get a little land which they can cultivate. He and the others had written to Mayawati for this purpose but there was no reply. 'Mayawati was in power but we did not get any benefit because we are few in number and so we are overlooked. The leaders who come to us for votes do not listen to us or understand us and don't take any action on our requests.'[3] (See Figure 2.1.)

From Sarju's narrative it emerges that although he and his family belong to the same caste as the Chamars of Shahabpur and thus have the same social identity, vote for the BSP like the Chamars of Shahabpur and thus have the same political identity, and follow the Ravidasi sect like them and thus have the same religious identity, they are still marginalized by the Chamars of Shahabpur who have shed their caste-based profession and have become visible in the social and political domain in recent years (Figure 2.2). Thus, in spite of having the same identity markers as the Chamars they are still denied equality. So what is the way out for them? Should we look at them by detaching them from all these identities and perceive them as a class? But class also forms a type of identity in the broader sense. Or we should try to find the path by combining the best of redistributive claims in terms of class issues and issues related to politics of

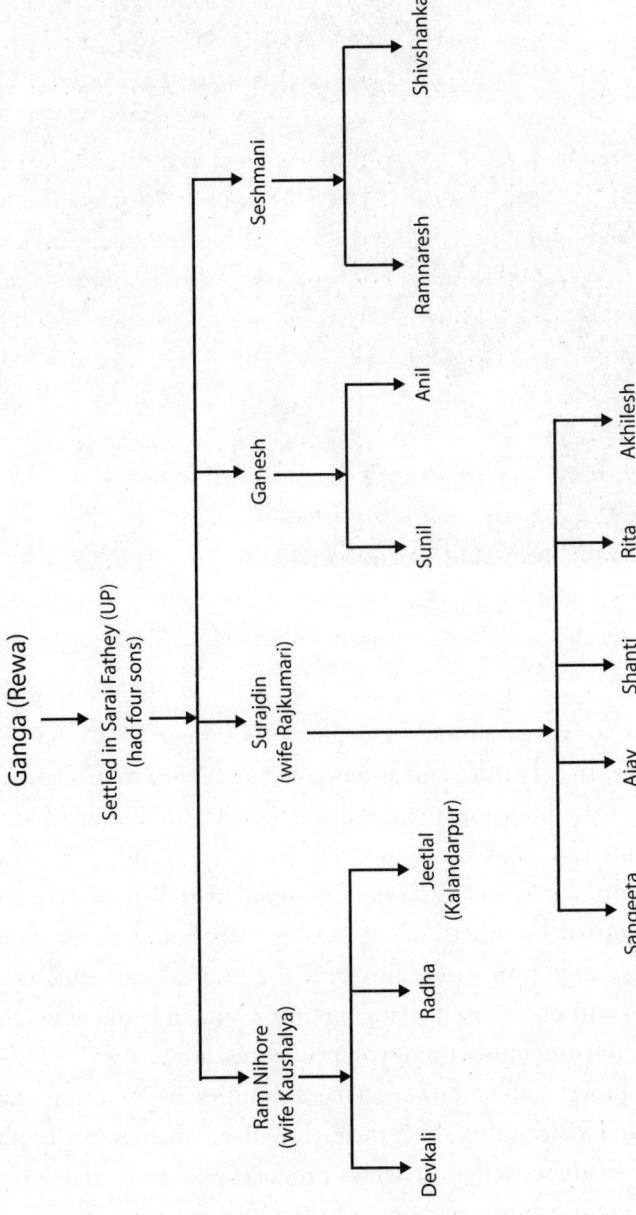

Figure 2.1 Family Tree of Sarju

Source: Based on field interview of Sarju by Brijendra Gautam in Village Shahabpur on 20 August 2012.

Figure 2.2 Sarju with His Children
Source: James Astill.

recognition as woven around caste identities (Fraser 1996). So how can Sarju get social justice and also become an agency to disseminate justice to others and not monopolize opportunities blinded by his own self-interest? How can he acquire the sense of pride (*garv*) to raise his social confidence, and not be humiliated, disrespected, and go unrecognized by others? How can his redistributive claims and politics of recognition make him gain the respect and equality of others, and without himself changing into a human being who consciously or unconsciously produces inequalities in society?

In the process of empowering communities by granting state resources and distributing them through welfare schemes, the implementation of these welfare schemes produces the sense of marginalization among various sections of society. In the next chapter we document the multiple experience of democracy in north Indian society through the narratives of the Musahars, a small dalit group in eastern UP.

Notes

1. Interview of Sarju by Brijendra Kumar Gautam, Shahabpur village, dated 16 December 2008.
2. Interviewed by Brijendra Kumar Gautam, Shahabpur village, dated 20 August 2012.
3. Interviewed by Brijendra Kumar Gautam, Shahabpur village, dated 20 August 2012.

3

Democracy, Deprivation, and Dispossession
Multiple Narratives of Democracy in North India

Our name is Musahar but we have no shahar (city)
How will we pass our lives?
In the hot afternoons we work hard
And our sweat streams down our faces
When we walk with wooden sticks tied on our shoulders
To sell them in the market
People laugh at us and give us less price
We have no place to live in the village,
No land to farm
And we are thrown outside the village
In the name of house
We have a small hut
In which mother-in-law, daughter-in-law
And all of us live together
We feed on water animals, snakes and rats
And hunt squirrels
Our empty stomachs force us to lick plates that have been eaten in

Along with dogs
When we are not allowed to cut leaves from trees
Then how can we make leaf plates to survive?
Earlier we used to bear the palanquins of brides and bridegrooms
But now motor cars have stolen this livelihood
Our bodies are covered with torn clothes
And we have nothing to cover ourselves with
On chilly nights we curl up like a ball
And keep ourselves warm with fire
Police call us from our houses and frame us in false cases
In jails we are forced to pick up dirt
And there is no one to listen to our woes
The country is free
But we are still slaves
There is no government for us
In such a state brother Mitai (the poet)
Please tell us how to cross the ocean

—Prasad (2007: 342)

This song, written by a person belonging to the dalit community, narrates the pathos and anguish of the Musahars and the pathetic manner in which they lead their lives. They are oppressed, ostracized, and exploited by everyone including policemen who frame them under false charges and make them clean the prisons. Leading lives of abject poverty and misery they somehow eke out an existence in this world. The poet rightly says that although the country is free they (and other marginalized communities like them) are still slaves.

This chapter documents the multiple experiences of democracy in north Indian society through the narratives of the Musahar community of eastern UP. These narratives of multiple marginalizations are crucial for understanding the articulation of the democratic experience by the weaker and marginalized sections of society. We explore how state-led categories, which had been developed by the state to bring equality in society, led to the maldistribution of resources and produced marginalization in several cases in Indian society. These articulations of marginalization of small dalit groups emerge through their everyday life in which they experience state-led democracy by its presence in the form of various aspects of social justice.

The Musahar is a community that is believed to be an offshoot of the Bhuiya tribe of Chhota Nagpur. To the community, the word 'musahar' signifies flesh-seeker or hunter (*masu* meaning flesh, *hera* meaning seeker). Some interpret it to signify rat-taker or rat-eater (from *musa* meaning rat) (Joshi and Kumar 2002: 20). Musahars belong to the Scheduled Castes and, according to the 1981 Census their total population in UP is 1,26,018. The Musahar of UP—also called Vanamanus, Banjara, or Gonrare—are mainly distributed in the districts of central and eastern UP. They are the most efficient soil cutters (Joshi and Kumar 2002: 13). According to Asharfi Sadai, 'The Musahar and earth are like a two in one' (Joshi and Kumar 2002: xvi). Their language is Awadhi.

The Musahars of Mirzapur are of an altogether different stock. In the local language, they are called *vanamanus*, which means forest dwellers. They collect honey and make *pattal*s (plates made of leaves). They are a tribal group, and were once hunter-gatherers who collected fruits and flowers from forests (Joshi and Kumar 2002: 139). They are mainly a landless community working as palanquin-bearers, agricultural labourers, or labourers in brick kilns, while some are involved in piggery. Modern developmental programmes have made only a little impact on them. While earlier, till 1995, the focus of the Indira Awaas Yojana (IAY) was directed on the Musahars only, this facility has now been extended to all SC castes and so the Musahars do not get proper housing facilities (Joshi and Kumar 2002: 96). Recent surveys indicate that the spread of education among the Musahars is extremely limited—just three per cent (Joshi and Kumar 2002: 1) According to the 1981 census, only 6.95 per cent of them are literate. In India, the average literacy rate of the Musahars was 52 per cent. Of this aggregate, 64.13 per cent were men and 39.29 per cent were women (Joshi and Kumar 2002: 90).

The homes of the Musahars are usually small 10 by 10 by 6 thatched huts (Joshi and Kumar 2002: 7). Goats, cows, oxen, and buffaloes are among the major livestock of these people (Joshi and Kumar 2002 49). Musahars are Hindus by name but other Hindus neither dine with them nor accept them into their social fold (Joshi and Kumar 2002: 70). They worship deities like Dudh Beer, Tulsi Beer, Deena Bhadari, and Shabari (Joshi and Kumar 2002: 144). However, they do not have pictures of these gods in their homes. Instead, they make objects of clay and worship these as symbols of their deities. They offer *kasar* or plantains to gods (Joshi and Kumar 2002: 148). The Musahars like singing, dancing, acting, and so on, and they drink liquor and consume pork which makes caste Hindus consider them 'debauched'.

The Musahars are an extremely marginalized caste and even after almost 60 years of post-colonial Indian democracy and governance they continue to languish on the fringes of society. In spite of being a part of state-generated development their experiences of democracy are quite different from the narratives of other dalit castes. In this chapter we document some narratives of Indian democracy by a few people belonging to the Musahar communities living in three villages of eastern UP near Varanasi. Our focus is to understand their relationship with democracy around the tangible presence of the developmental initiatives of the state in the form of housing, loans, education, employment, and livelihood initiated under state-made category-based schemes of development and social justice.

Experiencing Democracy: Myths and Realities

Our field research among the Musahars reveals that their low political visibility among dalit groups is because of their small population, lack of capacity to aspire to and acquire a better share in democracy, and their inability to produce community leaders. They feel as though they are still standing outside the circle of democratic benefits even among SCs. It is easy to note their confusion over the state-generated modernity that is reflected through the state-led frame of education, livelihood, and lifestyle. The first village that we studied was Dallipur. It is 12 kilometres from Varanasi, on the way to Jaunpur. The village profile shows a mixed-caste population with Kurmi (800 to 900 households), Musahar (250 households), Chamar (400 households), Gupta (100 households), Patel (200 households), and Brahmin (10 households). The village has a primary school, two wells, and four hand pumps. Inside the Musahar hamlet there is a pond called *Kajahariya Pokhar*. The pradhan of this village is of the Chamar caste. The Musahars live in their own hamlet called Musaharpatti.

The second village is called Anai and it lies in district Mangalpur. The village has a population of around 3,000. The land is good for farming and nearly 320 households are involved in this sector. A canal flows through this village and alongside there are also 50 tube wells with electricity connection. All households have electricity. There is a primary school in the village where children of all castes, including Musahars, study. The pradhan of this village belongs to the Patel caste. The village has a mixed caste composition with 2,800 Brahmin, 60 Musahar, 200 Chamar, 60 Khatik, 25 Muslim, and 200 Patel households. This village is totally illiterate but the children of the present generation have started going to school.

The third village is Jungalpur Kathiranv (Figure 3.1). The population of this village is nearly 22,000 with voter strength of about 15,000. This is a big village with a mixed caste composition. There are 1,500 Chauhan, 300 Musahar, 100 Baniya (Vaishya), 1,000 Patel, 100 Muslim, and 20 Yadav households. The pradhan of the village, Arun Kumar Gupta, belongs to the Vaishya caste, which comes under the OBC category. The village is connected to the main road and has

Figure 3.1 Musahar Village, Jungalpur, District Varanasi, Uttar Pradesh, India
Source: Brijendra Gautam.

health centres, 52 ponds, and eight schools. It has electricity, water supply and adequate irrigation facilities. All these infrastructural facilities make it appear as an ideal village.

To elicit oral histories the *baat se baat* methodology was employed and this involved extracting information from semi-structured conversation. The purpose was to identify persons of different ages with interesting narratives and an encyclopaedic memory of the past of the village, local history, culture, traditional knowledge, and so on. We chose three sets of individuals from each hamlet, including both men and women in order to note the variation in memory between the various castes, generations, and genders. The three age-groups were people above 70 years, those in their fifties or thereabouts, and those approximately 20.

We observed that the presence of state-led democracy in the everyday life of people works simultaneously in two ways. First, it makes them economically dependent on the state, and secondly, it makes them feel more deprived than other communities. Alongside, among the SC and ST communities, which have been provided special protective discrimination under the notion of social justice through various welfare measures, the communities that have the capacity to acquire and the capacity to aspire have attained a minimum level of development by appropriating a larger share of the welfare measures. In such a situation, many dalit communities receive only a small share of the benefits through the trickledown effect. However, even among these communities no common pattern is visible. Only the communities that have assertive organic leaders who can make claims on behalf of the community are able to get some share of the benefits. The form in which the claim is made is, however, like that of a subject (*praja*) placing his request (*fariyad*) before the king (*raja*), as Srinath, a member of the Musahar community, told us. In fact, the communities often use the word 'fariyad' when describing their appeals to the bureaucrats, who are the representatives of the state-led democracy. In such a situation it often appears that even today democracy has taken the form of kings and subjects, where the subjects place their requests (fariyad) before the king. The dalits communities that are able to increase their capacity to articulate such fariyads are able to claim a larger share of the democratic resources.

Claiming to be Poorest in Democracy

Musahar respondents began their narratives by trying to prove that they are the most marginal of all SC communities. As Srinath pointed out to us, *mushar se jyada garib kaun hai* (who is poorer than the Musahars?). However, it is interesting to learn that there are several communities who are as poor, if not poorer than the

Musahars. For example, the Kanjars, who live in the Kanjar *basti*, say very emphatically that they did not get anything from the sarkar. However, some nominal state benefits did reach them through the trickle-down effect and when they acknowledged that they were getting some benefits from the state they described themselves as being in a comparatively disadvantageous position in comparison with other OBCs and Dalit castes that are more visible in democratic politics.

The experience of democracy which emerges from the narratives of the Musahars seemed to be true even at the ground level if we analyse the structure of political parties working in this region. It is shocking to learn that there is no Member of Legislative Assembly (MLA) or Member of Parliament (MP) from this community even after more than 60 years of Independence. So if democracy means political participation they still hold one of the most disadvantageous positions even among dalit castes. While voicing their dissatisfaction over their limited political participation, Surmati, a 55-year-old woman from Musaharpatti in Dallipur village, says, 'Humro jati me abe tak kauno lal batti na mila ba bhaia (Our caste has yet to receive any "red beacon" car)'. Here, lal batti (red beacon light) signifies that the vehicle is for the conveyance of a minister.

If democracy means equal distribution of resources by the democratic state, they assert that they have no access to any of the welfare schemes launched by the government for the uplift of the downtrodden sections. The benefits of reservation make no sense for them. In Dallipur village, most of the Musahars are illiterate except for a lone 20-year youth, Rajkumar, who has passed his intermediate examination. Some of their children go to school but most of them don't pass high school. Many children drop out to become child labourers and supplement the family income. They usually work in agricultural fields, brick kilns, and so on. About 15 to 20 youths of this caste have migrated to Gujarat in search of work. In any case, the school near their hamlet provides education to the children only till class 5 and the children have to travel to other villages if they want to study further.

The people of this community still live in small, thatched huts. Their *patti* is like a village slum. This is a harsh reminder of the tangible and intangible artifacts of Indian democracy that have survived in the last 60 years in these villages. In the name of development there are some *pucca* (brick and concrete) houses in the village which were allotted in the 1980s under the Indira Awaas Yojana. However, the owners use these dwellings for rearing pigs, while they themselves live in mud huts. The reason for this is that they were told that these houses were too weak and fragile to stay in and could collapse anytime. Also, the houses have large windows through which they feel that ghosts and spirits can enter. On the other hand, their mud houses either have no windows or have very small ones. Ramrati, a 45-year-old woman of the Musahar community of Dallipur, district Varanasi, told us, 'When Indira Gandhi was alive we were given small houses. The houses have now broken down. We have never lived in those houses because ghosts and spirits can enter into them.'[1]

All the Musahars in the three villages complain that no one bothers about them as all the welfare schemes, including NREGA, are grabbed by other powerful castes. According to Surmati, the entire benefit of NREGA is taken away by the Thakurs, Brahmins, and Kurmis. 'Our men only drink and remain at home and there is no unity among them. This is the reason why, in spite of this being an SC seat, when Rajkumar, the only educated youth of this caste, contested the election of pradhan, the Musahars were divided in two groups and he lost. Instead, Sunnar Chamar, of the Chamar caste, won the polls,' she told us.[2]

The Musahars of this village had several complaints against Sunnar Chamar. According to them, before the elections he used to almost live in this hamlet but after winning the election he stopped bothering about them. Ramkali, a 65-year-old woman says, 'We do not get any benefit of the government's welfare schemes. No one listens to us.'[3] When we asked her why they do not meet political leaders and government officials, Ramkali remarked, 'The upper castes listen to the people of their own castes. No one listens to lower castes like us.'[4]

Although the Musahars of these villages are entitled to BPL (Below Poverty Line) or *Antyodaya* cards meant for the poorest of the poor to provide them food grains at highly subsidized rates from Fair Price Shops, they all have APL (Above Poverty Line) cards, under which they get food grains at higher rates. By no criteria can these poor Musahars be counted among the above poverty line. They say the village pradhan had assured them that they would be given the appropriate card later as their dream was to get the *lalka karad* (red Antyodaya card) and *ujarka karad* (white BPL card), whereas they have *piyarka karad* (yellow APL card). The Musahars of Dallipur village dwell around a pond called Kajahariya Pokhar. Despite their long-standing request for the lease (*patta*) of this pond, which is the main source of their sustenance and livelihood, they did not get it. The narrative of Ramsurat Baba (65 years), of Dallipur village, about Kajahariya Pokhar (pond) reveals the story of their marginalization by the postcolonial democratic state, through which the story of this marginalized community emerged.

> We have been living here for five generations. Cantonment Sahib brought our ancestors here and settled them in order to perform free labour on the landlord's land. Till now no land has been leased to the Musahars. The pond belonged to our ancestors but it has been forcibly taken away from us by the Kurmis. We have appealed to the higher officials for getting back our pond but there is no hearing.[5]

Rajkumar informed us that in order to get back their pond the Musahars had staged a demonstration in front of the DM's office but no action was taken. A little wasteland along the side of the pond is used by the Musahars. When the water of the pond rises and fishes are spawned there are regular skirmishes between the Kurmis and the Musahars over who will collect the fish to sell.

Narratives of Comparative Disadvantage

The narratives above deal with the feelings of the Musahars regarding the constant ongoing comparative dispossession from their livelihood sources and the poor quality of life in the modern democratic state. Battling against hunger they have forgotten their traditional cultural resources. When asked if they remembered their traditional folk songs, Phoolmati (55 years), of Dallipur village, said, 'Those who sit under fans and coolers can remember their songs. Our need is to fill our stomachs. We have no time to remember or sing any song.' Through their discourses it often appears that they feel that their past was better. Due to unequal distribution of democratic resources and malfunctioning of state-led schemes their economic and social conditions have further declined. According to the women of the community, 'Everyone is busy earning and eating. Who is concerned about the poor? All the leaders and officers come here, listen to our problems, give us false assurances and then leave.'[6]

In order to uplift the disadvantageous and poor communities in India there are provisions for bank loans at cheaper interest rates. In addition, there are many microcredit groups who with the help of National Bank for Agricultural and Rural Development (NABARD) in the region provide credit to poor people. However, even these loans meant for them are beyond their reach. Due to their illiteracy and ignorance they fear taking loans. Lallan (47 years) of Dallipur village, says,

> God knows on which paper they will make us put our thumb impression. In 1980, I took a loan of Rs 5,000, out of which Rs 800 was

taken away by the agent. With the remaining money I bought a pig but it died. I made no profit. All Thakurs and Brahmins take loans on our names. Their loans are written off.[7]

Thus when it comes to getting benefits in the state-led democracy they are totally deprived. All the benefits are usurped by the upper castes and dominant middle castes. Even during the BSP regime when Mayawati was the chief minister of UP and there was hope of developing a new Indian democracy with the inclusion of dalit and marginalized communities, they found no space. They have never existed in the polity or concerns of our democracy. They did not even get the benefits of ambitious projects like Ambedkar Gram Yojana for dalit villages during Mayawati's reign. Though the village fulfilled all the criteria for an Ambedkar village it was not categorized as such. Instead, the neighbouring village, which has a Chamar majority, wangled the said status.

When we asked the Musahars of Anai village whether they had taken any loan from the bank they replied in the negative. The reason was that the pradhan had told them that if they took a loan it would need five generations to repay it as the interest rates were high. Lalai, a resident of Anai added that even if they took a loan, the block office staff and the middlemen took away a large percentage of the money. If a loan of Rs 10,000 was taken nearly Rs 3,000 had to be paid as commission. Thus although they received only Rs 7,000 they had to pay interest on Rs 10,000. So, no Musahars applied for bank loans.[8] All the people from Musaharpatti accepted their poverty as their destiny. Unlike the people of Dallipur village they are silent about their rights. They somehow manage to exist in the village by performing various menial works. They have neither any agricultural land nor the traditional occupation of making leaf plates.

The residents here feel that they have got nothing substantial from Indian democracy. This caste, despite being SC, has not been able to develop the capacity to enjoy the caste status that they rightfully deserve. They have no visibility or voice that could draw the attention of the state or democracy towards them. The caste has neither the heroes nor the educated lot that are a must for visibility. They have no place in democracy as the development projects are far away from them.

While narrating experiences of everyday life in the village, Lalai of Anai village tells us that the Musahars lead very miserable and poverty-stricken lives. Earlier they used to earn their living by making leaf plates from mahua trees. The plates were supplied to various castes during weddings and other occasions. Now, however, plastic plates are available and so there is almost no demand for leaf plates. He added that the Musahars used to live in the jungles and were dependent on forest products but with large-scale deforestation their livelihood has been taken away. Today, they earn their livelihoods by working as labourers in the nearby fields.[9] This is a story of their dispossession in a democratic state.

Lalai told us that the Patels have a stronghold in the village and control the ponds. Sukhrani, a Musahar resident of this village stated, 'Earlier, we lived in the west of the village but when the population of Brahmins and Thakurs increased, we were pushed to the south of the village.' He added, 'We do not get any government money or benefits. Whenever some scheme is launched the upper castes grab all the money.'[10]

The women of the village say that they sometimes get some medicines, and a little ration from the fair price shop but they are not aware of the benefits to which they are entitled. In spite of various government welfare schemes for the uplift of the downtrodden sections, they suffer from poverty, hunger, and misery as they are outside the ambit of these schemes. Although they are all below the poverty line they have not been given BPL cards. After a lot of running round they were allotted the white APL cards. They only get a little wheat and rice with this card but do not get sugar, kerosene oil, palm oil, and so on. When the SP came to power, the Musahars were promised houses but although more than a year has passed they have still not been given houses. When they go to the government officials with their requests (fariyad), they are turned away.

The reason why their requests are not heard by the administration is that they do not have any leaders among them who can submit their fariyad to the sarkar (administration) in an effective way. No one in the village is literate. There is no one to fight for them and place their demands before the political leaders or the government. They have not yet developed their community leaders who can understand the state language and its *niyam-kanun* (rules and regulations) and are able to translate the state language into the community language. They have not yet fitted into the state-led pedagogic democracy.

Fariyadi Matters

The story of the Musahars in Jungalpur village is a little different. In this village there is a youth named Srinath who has emerged as a community leader. He is illiterate but articulate and has proved to be an effective *fariyadi* in a couple of cases that brought a few state benefits to all the Musahars of the village. As in Dallipur village, the Musahars of Jungalpur also did not have any right over the pond in the village since the Muslims had a 15-year lease on it. The Musahars ran from pillar to post to get the lease on the pond but to no avail. However, recently, after a long fight, Srinath succeeded in getting the lease. He told us how he obtained it, 'I had sent repeated requests and applications to the DM but there was no effect. One day I went straight to the DM's office and told him, "*Huzoor*, if you are the king of the government (*sarkar*), we are the king of the jungle. *Huzoor*, please give us one chance and see the result. Our wives and daughters do not have place to even throw the ashes of the stoves".'[11] The DM was impressed by Srinath and ordered tea for him. He gave him Rs 100 and promised to try to give him the lease on the pond. On the other hand, a man from the Muslim community of the village called Hyder Ali, who had the 15-year lease on the pond and used to rule over it, was, for his part, trying to get the lease extended. However, the DM supported Srinath and the Musahars were given lease on the pond for 10 years.

Since Independence, several Five Year Plans have been carried out and a large number of welfare schemes have been passed but this is the first time that the Musahars managed to get a lease of the pond. Before this, in 1982, the Musahars were allotted 11 houses under the Indira Awaas Yojana. During Mayawati's reign, 18 quarters were constructed and 28 households were given land on lease to build houses. However, they could not construct their huts on them since the land allotted to them by the pradhan was surrounded by Muslims. They did not allow the Musahars to settle there since the Musahars rear pigs, which the Muslims perceive as not only dirty and unclean, but unholy as well. The Musahars were unable to fight for land in some other part of the village since by that time Mayawati had been removed from power.

Another fariyad of Srinath about scholarships for Musahar children was also heard by local officials. He informed us,

> Since the Musahars are categorized as SC, when scholarships were distributed to OBC children in the school, the Musahar children were denied the scholarships. My son had told his mother that this time when the scholarships are given please buy me a pair of shoes. However, we were told that the scholarships were meant only for OBC children and the SC would be given scholarships later. After waiting for two months, the scholarships did not come. We felt bad since we had promised to buy shoes for our son. I was angry. I headed for Banaras to meet the DM with my *fariyad*. I said, "Sahib, I have brought a *fariyad*. We are Musahars, poor and illiterate. We are dying of hunger. My son goes to school. It is very cold but he goes bare-foot. The scholarships were distributed to OBC children again yesterday

after being distributed to them two months ago. The SC children were not given scholarships. If we had been given, we would have bought shoes for our children. It is very cold".[12]

The DM assured Srinath and the others of their village that they would get the scholarships within two days. However, this did not happen. After two months, when Srinath went to the DM's office again the DM recognized him. He asked Srinath if he had got the scholarships. When he replied in the negative the DM was angry. He called for his car and went to the village. There all the villagers again placed their fariyad before him and the other officers who had accompanied him. Soon after they were given the scholarships.[13]

Similar to the two other villages, the Musahars of Jungalpur have also not obtained the benefits of any government-loan schemes for the welfare of the poor and downtrodden sections. On asking the pradhan about the facility of obtaining loan, he replied that once someone took a loan from the government the person's sons and grandsons would not be able to repay it. It was because of this fear that most people did not avail themselves of the loans. However, some people did take loans. One of the experiences of taking a government loan was narrated by Lalai of village Dallipur. He said,

I applied for a loan for Rs 5,000 but got only Rs 4,000. The middle-men and agents pocketed the rest. I bought three pigs. Two died. I suffered a big loss as the interest increased and the bank officials kept asking me to deposit the interest. I am unable to pay the interest, let alone the principle. The bank officials and village panchayats in collusion do not give us the entire amount we apply for but we have to pay interest on the full amount. It is because of this fear that very few people take loans.[14]

While maintaining pride in their identity as 'king of the jungle' the Musahars claim their dispossession in modern state but alongside they also continue to disapprove in some sense the modern state defined life style. According to them, the reason they do not want to stay in the Indira Awaas Yojana houses allotted to them is that they see 'ghosts' in those houses and prefer to live in the jungle where they are happier.[15]

This chapter showed that the Musahars, who belong to the SCs and are one of the most marginalized dalit castes, have several complaints about state-led Indian democracy. While narrating these complaints and their experiences of democracy they continuously try to prove themselves as 'most poor,' and expressions like 'not getting anything from sarkar' appear again and again in their narratives. They feel that other castes that are dominant and powerful—whether upper, middle, or even other dalit castes, usurp their democratic rights and benefits. The Musahars do not have educated and assertive leaders who can present their fariyad to the local administration. They also do not have their own MPs or MLAs who can represent them in government. They hesitate taking loans under government schemes for the SCs and poor. They refuse to live in houses allotted to them under state given housing schemes because of the traditional notion of community habitat. Thus, in their experience, democracy raises aspirations but also gives rise to dissatisfaction. The state-sponsored schemes empower various communities but also make them more and more dependent on the state gradually. As diagnosed by Sudipta Kaviraj, 'state in the Indian context, as distinct from the European, has been the primary source of modernity. Even in the age of liberal economy the enchantment of state is still undiminished' (Kaviraj 2005: 2). Democracy in contemporary form in India has turned into state-led democracy or *sarkari cheez*. The political agencies expected to be involved in deepening democracy have turned their politics into 'gift politics' like distributing blankets, cheap rice, free tablets and *wajifa* (scholarship) for students, pension schemes, and so on. Thus political parties are not interested in the dissemination of the values of democracy but rather in distributing gifts to allure their subjects (*praja*) to mobilize them for elections. In this process, all the marginalized castes expect gifts from political parties, which is the only meaning democracy has for them.

It is a notable fact that the caste and communities among middle and dalit castes, which are numerically dominant, get more attention of the state and political parties as they comprise a larger vote bank. Those who have incorporated themselves well in the state-democratic logic of development and modernity through modern state-framed education, or have developed their caste leaders who can represent their demands to the state, get a larger share of the welfare projects of democracy. The castes that have not fully prepared themselves to be accommodated in democracy and in the modernity and development frame, suffer from a democratic deficit.

Despite low numbers, these castes should develop education and collective leadership within themselves that might strengthen the 'politics of presence' among them and give them a voice. However, as the post-modern thinker Derrida pointed out, 'Voice alone does not guarantee any presence.' Several other elements must be added to it. This would ensure that others do not drown their voices and present them in a wrong light. It is necessary that within the community, other than the aspiration for development, they should develop such elements that make them 'political'. Political scientist Rajni Kothari, noting the value of political consciousness among caste, had suggested that politicization of caste played an important role in the facilitation of democracy and the growth of social awareness (Dirks 2001: 286).

In the following chapter we will see how the state-led cultural policies, which include funding, have led to the suppression of the culture of dalit castes as a whole, and that among them there is a large section of dalit castes like the Sapera, Nat, Musahar, Pattharkat, Kanjar, and so on, whose culture is invisible even to other dalit castes.

Notes

1. Interviewed by Brijendra Gautam, village Dallipur, 4 March 2013.
2. Interviewed by Brijendra Gautam, village Dallipur, 4 March 2013.
3. Interviewed by Brijendra Gautam, village Dallipur, 4 March 2013.
4. Interviewed by Brijendra Gautam, village Dallipur, 4 March 2013.
5. Interviewed by Brijendra Gautam, village Dallipur, 4 March 2013.
6. Interviewed by Brijendra Gautam, village Dallipur, 4 March 2013.
7. Interviewed by Brijendra Gautam, village Dallipur, 4 March 2013.
8. Interviewed by Archana Singh, village Anai, 5 March 2013.
9. Interviewed by Archana Singh, village Anai, 5 March 2013.
10. Interviewed by Archana Singh, village Anai, 5 March 2013.
11. Interviewed by Nivedita Singh, village Jungalpur, 5 March 2013.
12. Interviewed by Nivedita Singh, village Jungalpur, 5 March 2013.
13. Interviewed by Nivedita Singh, village Jungalpur, 5 March 2013.
14. Interviewed by Brijendra Gautam, village Dallipur, 4 March 2013.
15. Interviewed by Brijendra Gautam, village Dallipur, 4 March 2013.

4

Margins and Politics

Narratives of Marginalized Dalit Castes*

Abhi main ichchhaen dharan karke kya karoon
Vyarth tomri bajake kya karoon
Sansar mein khamosh logon ki koi nahi sunta

(What is the use of nurturing desires at this moment.
Why should I play the *tomri* [subaltern musical instrument] uselessly?
In this world no one cares to listen to the words of the silent.)

—Sant Tukaram, *Abhang*

Who are the *people* who imagine the(ir) nation? How do the dalits or lower backward castes (especially the artisan communities called *ati dalit*) bearing caste-names like Banjara, Nat, Jogi, Daroga, Rawana, Rajput, Bharbhuja, Pinjara, Gariya, Luhar, Kachhi, Kasai, Dhobi,

---

* An earlier version of this chapter was published as 'Domination: How the Fragments Imagine the Nation: Perspectives from Some North Indian Villages', *Dialectical Anthropology*, 29(1): 123–40, New York: Springer, 2005.

Sapera, Baazigar, Khatik, Darzi, Kumhar, Chhipi, Rangrez, Thatera, Bhishti, and so on, imagine the nation? What is the meaning of the nation-community for these economically vulnerable and socially marginalized groups? Concurrently, how do the educated, mainstream dalits (the 'creamy layer' as the Hinglish jargon goes) with a fair amount of exposure to the media, imagine the nation?

These are the questions I try to confront in this chapter. I explore the perception of the nation among various dalit communities today and study how the 'past' circulates among them through the print media, and how the reality-effect of these narratives are generated and nurtured. I will also examine the role that the dalit press plays in transmitting ideas of the nation. I will try to show that the communities that are not exposed to the mainstream media and are not in the forefront of the competition for 'self-improvement' have a different story to tell: of the nation and of themselves.

The study is based on the narratives collected in two villages of Allahabad district, UP, where the spectacular rise of the long-oppressed dalits in the last two decades or so is being watched with great interest and concern. The first of these villages is Shivpuri, a village near the Meja tehsil, about 50 kilometres south of Allahabad. It is a small *patti* inhabited mostly by scheduled castes. The other village is Shahabpur, about 15 kilometres northwest of Allahabad, on the Lucknow Road, where people belonging to various lower as well as upper castes, live. The village is a conglomeration of 13 big caste-based pattis (hamlets) that are divided among the various upper, backward, and lower castes. In both villages I had extensive conversations with a number of people.

Imagination

In Shivpuri, the first person I met was a man called Nemi (age 50 years). Nemi belonged to the Bharbhuja caste (a community whose customary vocation is making puffed rice), whose members live on the periphery of the settlement of the lower castes in the south of the village. He is totally illiterate and can only put his thumb impression on paper. The two places he has visited in his life are pretty close to his own village—Meja and Karchhana. His everyday activities consist of chopping wood, collecting dry twigs and frying puffed rice for villagers. I sat down next to him and tried to draw him out in the folk dialect. On being asked about his idea of the nation, he replied: *Bhaiya, i des os hum ka jane. Hamre lel i gaonen—jawar des ha. Aur hum kuchh jada na jane.* [Sir, what do I know about the nation-tation. The village and its environs are my nation. This is all I know about this matter.][1] Exasperated, I asked him whether he knew something about Bharat (India). He knows nothing and he has no curiosity either. He wore a rather cold, impassive expression on his face.

The second person I met was Munnan Kasai (butcher), a sixty-year-old man of the same village. Predictably, he also knew nothing about the nation but he said that in the year 1971 (when a patriotic war was fought with Pakistan over the independence of Bangladesh and when patriotism was rampant), a Congressman called Ram Baran Upadhyaya came to the village and inspired him to sacrifice himself for the nation on the war front. Ever since, he has kept his sharpened knife (used for slaughtering goats) in readiness. He knows nothing about India or its capital, Delhi, which is only about 400 kilometres from his village. He does not know that there is such a thing called government headed by a prime minister. He believes that Rajiv Gandhi (long dead), the putative son of Mahatma Gandhi, is the present ruler of the country. About the freedom movement he had only heard about Ganhi (Gandhi) Baba. He had voted only twice since the 1950 general election, but did not know which party he had voted for. When asked about Murli Manohar Joshi, the well-known Bharatiya Janata Party (BJP) Member of Parliament (then minister in charge of Human Resource Development, Government of India) from that constituency, he said that he had heard his name and believed that he belonged to Rajiv Gandhi's party (in actual fact, the BJP is the rival of the Congress party).[2]

In the same village, there were some roving snake charmers (Gani Sapera) who go from house to house in the village, making their snakes dance to the music of the flute and receiving a little rice and wheat in exchange. After collecting the day's earnings, all the snake charmers gather at the *chaupal* (the common space in the centre of the village), to rest under the shade of a tree. I sat with them and tried to pick their brains about the nation. They replied laconically, *Kya sahab, jahan jahan ghoomte firte hain vahin to apna desh hai.* [Well, sir, wherever we go, there is our nation.] (Figure 4.1.)

Figure 4.1   Sant Raj Sapera, Leader of Kapari Village, Shankargarh Sapera Community
Source: Brijendra Gautam.

In the same village, I met Ram Baran (age 35 years), an inhabitant of the *Chamar patti* (a settlement of the Chamars, one of the lowest castes in the caste hierarchy).[3] He has a university education, is a graduate teaching in a private school in an adjoining village, and was very much aware of the Indian freedom struggle and the 'nation'. He subscribes to two newspapers, *Majhi Janta* and *Bahujan*, both with 'progressive' dalit affiliations. One of the leitmotifs of these newspapers is the (unacknowledged) role of the dalits in the Indian freedom struggle and in the making of the nation. This they do to stake a claim on public life in India today, which is, or was until recently, conspicuous by the absence of dalit figures. Ram Baran is an enthusiastic reader of the dalit press and disseminates the narratives to other dalits. Booklets (published after 1960) about the role of dalits in Indian history form a part of his personal library. He says that he acquired awareness and historical sense through these books and newspapers.[4] The crucial component of Ram Baran's 'nation' is a historic betrayal: the dalits built the railway lines, factories and other infrastructure only for these to be appropriated by the upper castes. The dalits have been completely marginalized in the dominant narratives as well as in realpolitik.

Notwithstanding Ram Baran's trenchant critique of the status quo, we must not think that dalitness is the natural outcome of the historic injustices meted out to the dalits. The academic study of marginalized or subaltern groups often suffers from this lacuna: one simply assumes that victimhood would lead to protest. I have studied the dalit movements and mobilizations in post-Independence north India (Narayan 2004) and I have shown in my earlier works how dalitness is *constructed* and *produced* through mobilizations and discourses. There is nothing 'natural' about it. The dalit snake charmers, puffed rice sellers, butchers, and so on, are not simply aware that dalitness is a subject-position that could give them some agency. They cannot because the temporality of the state has not impinged heavily into their everyday lives which, despite all epochal changes in modern India, have not yet broken with the archaic patterns of the village community's self-sufficiency and relative isolation. At some level, therefore, the solidarity of the oppressed *qua* oppressed subjects is *constructed* and a certain kind of oppression—the kind that calls for acting together to build what Kaviraj has called 'enumerated identity'—is not something people are aware of immediately. It is something fabricated (Kaviraj 1993). In ways which are familiar to the readers of Benedict Anderson's classic *Imagined Communities*, 'print capitalism', that is, the mediation of print culture, is crucial for constructing dalitness as identity, as we will see shortly (Anderson 1991).

The Enigma of Origin

Foucault, following Nietzsche's critique of morality, has reminded us about the murkiness of the Origin (Foucault 1977). Genealogy–Foucault's preferred name for a reflexive, critical history—shows that what seems noble and uplifting, actually originated in something crude and base: in the craving for power, for example. It was the privileged, educated dalits, wanting a share in power of the newly independent nation, who started the agenda of dalit awakening. The first step towards that was building up a dalit press—a network of print communication connecting would-be dalits in distant *mofussil* towns and villages in a common bond of dalitness. This is not to say that dalitness was invented from nowhere. As we will see below, in their traditional (unwritten) caste histories, myths and oral cultures, there was an acute awareness in each dalit caste of their marginalization, victimhood, and so on. Their caste histories contain narratives condemning the injustice of this state of affairs. But all this was done under the hegemony of the Brahminical discourse, which means that each dalit caste claimed that their degradation was accidental, and contingent rather than necessary. Further, there was nothing in the traditional discourse of the dalits that secured a generalized dalitness for all the dalits. So, there was no question of acting *together* as one body. Kaviraj has justly called this a 'fuzzy' sense of identity (Kaviraj 1993). We are about to witness how from this fuzziness, a modern, enumerated identity emerges through the inclusive modern politics of democratization.

Intervention and Representation in Print

The post-Independence Indian state is developmentalist and to take the opportunity of its developmental programmes one needs to organize and represent oneself to the state through the politics of mobilization. The nature of democracy that is operative in India is still quite imperfect and unorganized sections, however deserving, do not get the state's backing. Consequently, the first step to Dalit mobilization was consciousness raising which the literate section started doing by producing propaganda literature in print to sensitize and mobilize the masses. In this process, they had to interpret nationalism and Indian history from a 'dalit' point of view because it was only by becoming an interest-group within India's body politic that they could claim special privileges for themselves in the form of affirmative action by the state. One of the ways of going about it was to publish their own newspapers and, subsequently, to build up a dalit public sphere.

The dalit movement started in Maharashtra around 1877 through the efforts of Jyotiba Phule and Gopal Baba Walangkar. Ambedkar reasserted the dalit movement in the twentieth century around the year 1920. And, from the very beginning, publication and propaganda received top priority. Phule started a dalit newspaper called *Deenbandhu* on 1 January 1877 which, subsequently, proved to be quite influential. Between 1910 and 1930 there were nearly 50 newspapers published by Dalits all over Maharashtra of which *Bital Vidhwansham*, *Son Vanshiya Mitra*, *Nirashrit*, *Hind*, *Nagrik*, and so on, are well-known examples. Dr Ambedkar himself edited important dalit newspapers like *Janata* and *Mooknayak*. In the Hindi region, Swami Acchutananda was the first to publish a Hindi newspaper called *Achhut* in 1917. In 1928, he launched another newspaper called *Adi Hindu Mahasabha*. In 1934, a Hindi weekly newspaper called *Samta* was launched from Almora by Munshi Hariprasad Tamta. After Independence a flood of newspapers was started all over UP by the dalits themselves. From Aligarh, a fortnightly newspaper called *Parivartan* was started under the editorship of Ajudhyanath Dandi. In 1957, a newspaper called *Sinhnaad* was launched by Dayanand Vyas, who appointed Sunderlal Sagar, an eminent dalit writer, as the editor.

From the 1960s onwards, dozens of small, locally based newspapers started coming out. *Zamin ke Tare* was started in 1962 by Shri Sewaram Mahashaya, a freedom fighter from Aligarh; it was edited by Mishrilal Deepak, who also started a printing press in 1966 called Bhim Printing Press. In 1966, a newspaper called *Shoshit Pukar* was started from Bulandshahar with a print order of 1,000 copies. In 1968, *Swadheen Bharat*, a weekly newspaper was published from Aligarh. In 1972, *Samta Shakti*, a weekly newspaper, and in 1981, *Bahujan Adhikar*, a fortnightly newspaper, were started from Meerut, both edited by Mohandas Naimishrai. In 1978, Dr R.S. Azad started a six-page weekly from Bulandshahar called *Lok Chinta*, priced at only 40 paise. In 1982, another weekly called *Bheembhumi* was started from Bulandshahar. Nirnayak Bheem, a monthly newspaper was started from Kanpur, edited by D. Kawaldhari. Many famous dalit activists of the 1970s and 1980s such as Periyar Lalai Singh, Dr R. Kamal, Dr Motiram Shastri, Chandrakumar Varathe, and so on, wrote for these monthly magazines. The first daily newspaper of the dalits was started in 1985 under the editorship of Sri Durga Prasad. By the 1990s, the market was flooded with daily, weekly, fortnightly, and monthly newspapers and magazines. This phenomenon was an offshoot of the Mandal Commission, through which the dalits used their own mouthpieces to express their views and counterviews. Some of the newspapers that still exist today are: *Bahujan Digdarshak* (Lucknow), *Ananya Bharat* (Mainpuri), *Bhim Sainik* (Meerut), and *Dalit Chetna* (Lucknow). Some other Dalit papers were: *Mookbharat, Dalit Kesri, Dalit Jan Udgar, Lakshya Sandhan, Apana Abhiyan, Adhikar Bharti, Baudh Bandhu, Nag Times, Shoshit Samta, Shoshit Darpan, Kalyan Kutumb, Apni Rae, Guruvani, Durbal ki Awaz, Garima Bharati, Dalit Asia Today, Samaj Gauravi, Priya Sampadak, Kailash Bharti* (Lucknow), *Nidar, Savdhan, Kiranon ka Basera* (Saharanpur), *Samta Sandesh* (Ghaziabad), *Bheem Bharti* (Ghaziabad), *Arjak* (Lucknow), *Jhalkari Sandesh* (Agra), *Aitihasik Chhalang* (Saharanpur), *Prajapati Tarang* (Kanpur), *Rajat Bandhu* (Jaunpur), *Balmiki Prakash* (Allahabad), *Dard ki Duniya* (Ghazipur), *Dalit Prakash* (Kanpur), *Utthan* (Lucknow), *Budh Updesh* (Moradabad), *Bahujan ka Bhaichara* (Badaun), *Republican Inqalab* (Hapur), *Ambedkar Vikas Patra* (Vilari), *Bahujan* (Lucknow), and *Pragya Sahitya* (Farookhabad).

These newspapers, magazines, and other printed literature were the making of a microscopic literate section of the dalits. They were the opinion makers, community leaders and social activists. The newspapers were published daily, weekly, and monthly with print orders varying from 1,000 to 10,000. The newspaper *Bahujan Sangathak* is the party organ of the BSP and plays an important role in constructing popular perceptions among dalits. The number of readers is much larger than the number of subscribers since one copy is read by, and often read aloud to, many people. Ram Baran of Shivpuri village pointed out that the two newspapers subscribed by him, namely *Majhi Janata* and *Bahujan Samaj*, are borrowed, read, and discussed by many of the dalits living in that village.[5]

Initially, the newspapers were started by the aware, educated, mostly urban and salaried section of the dalits. The dalit elite, which had a strong urge for power sharing, combining with a slowly growing middle stratum of dalit population, started the struggle for a share in the fruits of the welfare schemes and other special benefits. More or less the same thing happened in UP, Maharashtra, and in some of the other Indian states. The gap between the dalit elite and the common dalit population also widened. While the dalit elite started imitating the lifestyle of upper-castes, the grassroots dalit population remained stagnant. This differentiation is more apparent in western UP where the Republican Party of India (RPI) is active mainly among the salaried class and urban dalits. However, the new dalit movement that emerged under the leadership of Kanshiram (BSP) managed to build up a dialogue and interaction between the urban elite, the natural leaders of the community, and the mass of rural and mostly illiterate dalits. The process of differentiation has become faster in the recent decade, though Kanshiram and his heir, Mayawati, represent the voice of almost all sections of dalits by integrating the interests of the elite, the middle section, and the grassroots dalit population in the BSP which has established almost a monopoly of dalit votes in UP and elsewhere. The electoral gains of the BSP in recent years are primarily responsible for increasing the tempo of propaganda and has seen to the avalanche of printed dalit literature in recent years.

Print, Perceptions, and Types

The spread of print-culture among dalits, whose history I have sketched roughly above, resulted in the formation of what can be called the *dalit public sphere*. Interestingly, they call this public sphere *parh-likh ke* (literal meaning: through reading and writing). But *parh-likh ke* no longer means just reading and writing—it has become a metaphor meaning the new identity of dalithood. Even the illiterate narrate their version of the suffering and oppression imposed on them by the dominant section by saying that they had come to learn about it by *parh-likh ke*. When they narrate their own personal experiences, they often say that they acquired these experiences through *parh-likh ke*. The phrase *parh-likh ke* is capable of lending legitimacy to almost anything connected with the new consciousness of dalitness. This usage is thus a tacit or not-so-tacit admission that the new dalit identity was fabricated through writing, discourse, newspapers, and books. What is compelling in the testimonies I have collected about dalitness, is their valorization of written knowledge and modern forms of discourse originating in political mobilizations and so on. There is also an undertone here that must not be missed: once written discourse and political discourse were parts of the mimetic capital of the upper-caste elite; after the recent awakening, these have been snatched away from them.

Let us give a hearing to the dalits of Shahabpur, a village near Allahabad. Narrating the past of his caste (Chamar), Pyarelal (age 76 of Godampatti, Shahabpur) said,

> I'm Pyarelal. I want to tell you about the past of the Chamars. Earlier *jhakhar*s (long grass reeds used for sweeping floors) were tied around our feet to clean the ground where we walked. In case a few footprints got left behind, the upper castes used to walk down the road only after the wind or an animal had cleared those away. When our children went to school, they were made to sit directly on the floor while the upper castes sat on mats. When our children drank water, they were cautioned not to touch the *lota* (vessel) or it would become polluted.[6]

Here is his version of the story of the origin of the Chamars:

> Once upon a time, Brahmins and Chamars were *sagey bhai* (real brothers). One day sage Ashtavakra (whose body was distorted at eight places) went to the house of the Brahmins for *godaan* (the ceremony of donating cow). He was given a cow as gift but he refused saying that he would not take anything. Some of the Brahmins then started deriding him for his distorted body. The angry sage cursed the

Brahmins by saying that since they were laughing at the *haar-maans* (bones and flesh) of a person, they would have to work with *haar-maans* all their lives. These Brahmins then became Chamars whose caste-occupation is to skin dead animals and remove their bones. This is how the Chamars originated.

Asked as to how he came to know all these, he replied, 'parh-likh ke' although he was totally illiterate.[7]

Among the Chamars living in the Godampatti of the Shahabpur village, the memory of their oppressive past has become enlivened through *parh-likh ke*. Jhuria, an old Chamar woman, vividly described the oppressions she suffered when she was young and worked in the Raja's house.[8] When Chamar women went to the Raja's bungalow to work, the members of the household did not look at their faces while talking to them. While grinding wheat and *makara* on the stone *janta*, a laborious job, they were made to tie pieces of cloth around their feet so that their sweat did not fall into the powder. Bells or *jhanjhar* were tied around their feet to warn people of their movements. After a hard day's work they were given five 'paus' of *jau* or *matar*. They were not given any money. Again she invoked *parh-likh ke* when asked how she remembered all this that had taken place long ago. She herself was illiterate but her husband and children and other villagers had some *parh-likh ke*. It is clear that she would not have found these narratives worth recalling without the backdrop of the movement.

Another narrative is that of Bhullar, a 50-year-old resident of Godampatti, a Chamar by caste who is semi-literate. He is a follower of the Ravidasi sect, a sect very popular among Chamars of eastern UP and Bihar. He tried to narrate a history of the past glory of the Chamars and their present fallen state.

Chamarvansh [Dynasty of Chamars] ruled over the entire subcontinent for the last one lakh seventy eight thousand years. According to the genealogical tree, all the great Hindu mythological figures like Supak Das, Ravi Das, Harish Das, Mor Dhwaj, Eklavya and so on, belonged to the Shudra Gotra. All the Rishi-Munis (sages and saints) were born in the Shudra caste. Only a few Rishis were from the Brahmin and Kshatriya castes. Balmiki and Parashar were also Shudras. King Ashoka was also a Shudra. His pillar is still *ajar amar* (intact).

'It so happened,' he continued,

that some clever invaders [Muslims] came to our country. Taking advantage of our ignorance they snatched away our *dhan dharm* (wealth and religion). We were forced to retreat in the forests and we had to eat the flesh of animals to pacify our hunger. When King Rana Pratap lost the battle, he also sought refuge in the forest. At that time our ancestors took care of him and later he won the battle with our help. But we did not get anything out of him. Even after the birth of Bhimrao Ambedkar, our people had to face the wrath of the upper castes. Ambedkar was not also allowed to touch the tap for drinking water. He had to struggle hard to obtain his education but he did not lose heart. Then an Englishman, who loved him, took him to his country. There Ambedkar continued his education and with his knowledge, changed the course of history and of our lives. The births of Ravidas and Ambedkar were a great blessing for the lower castes. We now have the right to education. We can get jobs. We can now sit and chat with you. But still much remains to be done.

On being asked how he knew so much, he replied assertively, 'Sahab, we have studied. We have read books. We spend time in the company of Sadhus. We go to Sabha Samaj (caste meetings, political rallies). We buy books from there. All this is written in books. A member of the BSP, Lalji Premi, visits our village often and distributes books and pamphlets.'[9]

From Bhullar's testimony, it is clear how information contained in the dalit press (mostly written by educated elite dalits), has permeated through semi-literate people like Bhullar to illiterate people like Jhuria and Pyarelal. The meaning of *parh-likh ke* now emerges clearly. Learning about what is written in the books from their semi-literate caste-brethren, the illiterate can then confidently claim that this is their own knowledge. Knowledge also comes from political mobilizations: sabhas and from *sadhus* which means wise people of the community. Thus traditional oral knowledge is imbricated with modern textual knowledge and print-capitalism is feeding oral community knowledge with modern notions of identity. This mixing of the high and the low is clearly discernible in Bhullar's testimony which is an attempt to weave various contradictory and fragmented narratives into a coherent whole to make it one story of dalit suffering and struggle. There is a conscious effort to project a history of the struggle of Chamars as a *shudra struggle* and a *bahujan struggle*. Here many different identities overlap, contradict and merge with each other. To my utter surprise, in course of six- to seven-hour-long sessions going on for five or six days, nobody ever used the term 'dalit' (the umbrella term under which the elite leadership wishes to bring in all the low castes to coalesce into a single political and electoral bloc), although terms like chamar, shudra and bahujan were used quite often. This shows that the rural folk do not merely repeat what comes to them through print but they use it staying within their own cosmology.

While Bhullar was talking about an umbrella identity of the Shudra, he could not forget their old feud with another dalit caste called the Pasis. The Pasis came up during his narration of their Naramaveshi Andolan in the 1960s when they refused to follow their traditional degrading caste occupation of leather tanning and removing the carcass of dead animals in order to purify themselves for rising in the caste hierarchy. He said,

> About forty or fifty years ago we stopped working on our traditional caste profession and our women stopped doing their polluting work

of delivering babies. When we tried to stop these activities, everybody, including the other lower castes, tried to convince us not to do so. The Patels were in the forefront of this agitation. When we searched for alternative work as agricultural labourers, they started beating us up and stopped us from using the roads. They did not allow us to drink water from the common wells and shunned us completely. The lowly Pasis, who are today allied with us in the BSP, also joined the Patels in forcing us to continue with our leatherwork. Those were real bad days. We revolted against the Patels and the Pasis. Four Patels went to jail as a result of our protest. At that time Bhurelal was the District Magistrate of Allahabad. When we complained to him, he asked us why we wanted to leave our traditional work. We explained that since animals did not die every day, it was difficult for us to sustain ourselves. We needed an alternative profession. Bhurelal then pacified us by saying that nobody can force you to do some work. From then on our social reform (*samaj sudhar*) became effective.[10]

He went on to say that this work of skinning dead animals was now being done by people who were brought to their village from Bilaspur.

We do not know whether they are members of our caste or not. They might be Chamars but we do not include them in our society. We do not allow them to eat with us and we segregate them. We try to live the way the people of higher communities live.[11]

Most of the Chamars of Godampatti have converted into Ravidasis and Kabirpanthis and have become vegetarian. They believe that this is important for attaining a higher caste status. On the other hand, the Pasis living in the Pasiyapur Patti say that one of the causes of the degradation of the lower castes is that they started eating cooked food. Khichrilal Pasi (55) of Pasiyapur village narrated the mythological story about degradation that came from eating cooked food. Rishi Parashuram enjoined them to adhere to the practice of eating uncooked meat while Narad Muni initiated them into eating cooked meat, which ultimately led to their fall. Thus, 'fall' is rationalized in terms of contingency and chance rather than the rational logic of cause and effect. They themselves were not responsible for their 'fall', it happened by chance and coincidence.[12]

All these three respondents, Pyarelal, Jhuria, and Bhullar are from Shahabpur village, which is only 15 kilometres from Allahabad. It is a stronghold of the BSP and its residents are politically more aware than those of the villages in the interior. It is possible that these interior villages—less influenced by the politics of dalit mobilization—may have more spontaneous, multiple, and more fragmented traditional narratives. These may project different kinds of protest through narrative production than the homogeneous kinds of narratives that are being circulated through printed literature, sabha-samaj, and so on, and are sought to be made coherent and more politically correct.

Dalit Communicators and Narrative Types

We just had an interface with the grassroots who are at the receiving end of things—they are receptors of the message spread by the dalit intellectuals and activists who are literate, articulate communicators: editors, writers, and social and political leaders. Our knowledge of the dalit public sphere would remain incomplete and tentative if we do not acquaint ourselves with a cross-section of these people. Most of these people active in the domain of printed discourse are 'organic intellectuals' with a missionary zeal for uplifting the communities with whom they have direct contact and communication. Their solidarity with the grassroots makes their messages easier to percolate down to the common and even illiterate dalits. One such organic intellectual is Shri Sohan Lal Shastri, a living legend among dalits, who spent 25 years with Ambedkar and contributed hugely in raising dalit awareness in the Hindi-speaking region. Another person is Mohan Kumar Nathu Singh Tawar, who has been publishing *Koli Rajput*, a dalit monthly, for the last 54 years. He also opened many schools for dalit children. Jay Ram Singh, a lawyer by profession, is the editor of *Dalit Jyoti*. He started his career as a roving seller of popular books, taught himself to read and write and went on to earn a university degree and was very active in RPI politics. There are many others like him in the long list of dalit communicators I interviewed—Jayram Prasad Singh, Kawal Bharati, Mata Prasad Sagar, and so on. Unlike ordinary Indian politicians, what is peculiar about dalit mobilizers in UP is that they combine various roles (schoolteacher, writer, propagator, journalist, and so on) into one. They also consider their vocation as a sort of mission. There are at least a few thousand such people in BAMCEF (Backward and Minority Communities Employees Federation) in UP. They act as a kind of go-between: they propagate the messages of the dalit press and books to unlettered dalits.

Speaking very broadly, the narratives we have collected from the ordinary and mostly illiterate dalits of Shahabpur and Shivpuri about what they understand by dalit awakening (as opposed to what is offered in writing in dalit books, pamphlets, and newspapers) can be grouped in two broad categories. These categories can be traced back to the mature Indian nationalism of pre-Independence India where there were distinct divergences between two different kinds of imaginations of the nation: the Gandhian and the Ambedkarite. Recently, in the course of critiquing Benedict Anderson's 'classical' model of nationalism as opposed to what he considered its inferior, adulterated and Third World variant—ethnic nationalism—Partha Chatterjee noted a fundamental disjuncture and heterogeneity as constitutive of the (Indian) nation's time (Chatterjee 2001). Now, in the narratives I have found among ordinary dalits, these two types of imaginations are sometimes separate, and sometimes mixed with each other. These are thus two archetypes or models of the Indian nationalist, one dominant and the other (the Ambedkarite) emergent. In dalit imagination today, however, the Ambedkarite version is increasingly becoming dominant while the Gandhian version is gradually fading.

The Gandhian imaginary was basically inclusive though it had space for the dalits and even the untouchables whom Gandhi called harijan. Gandhi started journals like *Harijan* (English) and *Harijan Sewak* (Hindi) in 1933 to address the cause of the dalits. In 1932, he founded the 'Harijan Sewak Sangh' to bring the dalits and lower castes into the mainstream. Around the same time, B.R. Ambedkar started propagating a different vision of dalithood through his news-paper *Janata*, which stressed the dalit's *difference* from the mainstream 'nation'. Ambedkar demanded a separate dalit space, rather than a submersion of the dalit cause in the Gandhian agenda of building a coherent, homogeneous nation-space. After the closure of *Janata*, he founded a series of newspapers like *Mook Nayak*, *Vahishkrit Bharat*, and *Prabudh Bharat* to further his cause of dalit nationalism. Self-consciously, Ambedkar was using the term 'depressed' for the low-castes and the untouchables while Gandhi was using the term 'Harijan'.

Gandhi's posture was that of uplifting the dalits: the upper castes were to be benign and tolerant towards dalits, and the dalits were to stop considering themselves as degraded and think of themselves as people of god (*harijan*). In this way he tried to link the lower castes with mainstream nationalism. The idea was to forge a broad-based, anticolonial front where differences within the nation would obviously be of secondary importance. In effect, the Gandhian attitude was that of pity towards the harijan. Gandhian writers like Maithilisharan Gupt, Biyogi Hari, and Ghanshyam Das Birla, who regularly wrote in the newspaper *Harijan*, simply wanted their (upper-caste) readers to be moved by the plight of the dalits.

As opposed to this politics of pity, which, it was hoped, would act as a kind of bond between the marginalized dalits and the main-stream, the prophet of the dalits, B.R. Ambedkar, wanted to fracture the very idea of a unified Indian nation as envisioned by Gandhi. He projected the heterogeneity of the nation-people. The attainment of social freedom for the dalits was more important than the political freedom of the nation. In fact, the Independence of India was justified on the grounds that without this precondition, dalit liberation would remain unattainable. Dalits must subvert the Brahminical social order and create the conditions for a modern citizenry (Ambedkar 1937).

Recurrence and Imagination

The story of dalit awakening through Ambedkar's pioneering efforts and exemplary leadership, his conflict with Gandhi, the Poona Pact, and the subsequent trajectory of dalit politics in Maharashtra and, more recently, after the Mandal Commission, in the whole of north India, has been told and retold many times. Serious academic scholarship on recent dalit history has usually phrased it as dalit assertion or a mass upsurge as against the upper-caste/class reaction manifested in the form of a certain hardening of right-wing Hindu fundamentalism (the rise of the BJP and so on). What is missing in this account and what I have been wanting to show throughout this account is the constructedness of the dalit identity and the manufacturing of a pan-Indian 'imagined community' of dalits through the print media and propaganda. Since all identities are constructed rather than primordially given, there is nothing wrong in creating a political agenda based on the construction of an identity of the oppressed. I have also tried to show that ordinary illiterate or semi-literate dalits do not just passively accept what is handed down from above but try to reconcile that with their existing fragmentary narratives of oppression based on very different resources like traditional oral caste histories and myths. Whenever I talked to such people about their identity, some excesses crept in which were not there in the official, politically correct discourse called *parh-likhe ke*.

Just how constructed the neo-dalit identity is can be shown by an example. In the autobiographical narratives I/we have collected, certain motifs recur with great regularity and frequency. There is little reason to doubt that these recursive motifs have come from *parh-likhe ke* rather than from the quotidian life-world of the individuals interviewed. These motifs are: 'tying mops around the feet', 'faced animal-like behaviour by forward castes', 'eating of flesh of dead animals due to poverty', 'picking out grains of wheat and rice from cow-dung or dustbins', and so on. In the post-Independence dalit print literature, we find exactly similar motifs as occurring in the lives recounted there. *Paon me jhakhar bandhana* (tying mops around the feet) is a frequent motif found in Marathi dalit printed autobiographies and reportage. In 1968, in an editorial published in the Marathi journal *Republican Bharat* and titled, 'Swaraj adhoora hai', we find the following quotation from a Chamar's interview:

> In my family I have a wife and four children. We remove dead cattle from the village. Just last month only two heads of cattle died in the village. From the sale of the leather we obtained four rupees, and by making two pairs of shoes for the villagers we made a profit of three rupees. From doing other kinds of labour, we received eighteen rupees. Thus we have to survive on a total of rupees twenty-five, which is insufficient to fill the stomachs of six people. That is why the entire family has to eat the flesh of dead animals.[13]

After citing this harrowing account, the editor went on to conclude that without creating a casteless and classless society, India's independence is incomplete.[14] More such examples can be found in the printed literature of the 1950s and 1960s.

The narrative types that emerge about the individual and collective pasts from the grassroots, from people like Jhuria, Bhullar, Pyarelal, Ram Baran, and so on are also found to recur consistently in the print literature of the dalits. We might call these archinarratives. Penned by the educated dalits, these have slowly permeated the dalit public sphere through recent sensitization and awareness programmes. The illiterate dalits at the grassroots who come under the transmission zone of printed narrative use this secondary memory as a resource for negotiating a relationship with the nation. Since memory is always (re)constructed rather than simply given by the past, it is already quite difficult to distinguish in the testimonies I have collected how much it is their 'own' memory and how much is extrapolated from the printed literature that offers a sketch of a collective past—a community myth. In the case studies mentioned above, the to and fro movement of the narratives from oral to printed and printed to oral can be discerned quite easily. It can also be seen how with the expansion of literacy, awareness, and mobilization, a politics of homogenization of the dalits is emerging. This is precisely what Ian Hacking has characterized as 'Making Up People' (Hacking 1986).

However, there is no need to think that the collective past manufactured by discourse and interaction is a static pool. On the contrary, the narrative types that appear as progressive today may turn out to be oppressive tomorrow. It is possible that the Bilaspuris, who have now taken over the profession of removing the carcass of dead animals, would be expelled from the narrative type related to the 'nara maveshi movement' as mentioned by the Chamars of Godampatti of Shahabpur, when these Chamars find out that the Bilaspuris are their comrades in their collective fight for dignity. Perhaps in future the Chamars of the Godampatti, while narrating the story of their conversion to vegetarian food, would suppress the narrative of Khichrilal Pasi implying that the degradation of the Pasis was due to their eating cooked meat. So long as the dalits continue to remain a people whose subjectivities are fractured and aligned with various layers of contested identities, 'small voices' would continue to make their troubling presence felt. I hope I have been able to do justice to them.

Notes

1. Nemi, interviewed by Sailesh Upadhyaya, village Shivpuri, 6 August 2001.
2. Munnan Kasai, interviewed by Sailesh Upadhyaya, village Shivpuri, 6 August 2001.
3. Ram Baran, interviewed by Sailesh Upadhyaya, village Shivpuri, 6 August 2001.
4. Ram Baran, interviewed by Sailesh Upadhyaya, village Shivpuri, 6 August 2001.
5. See the project report *Imagining Past: Memory, History and Development*, G.B. Pant Social Science Institute, Allahabad, 2003,
6. Pyarelal, interviewed by Sailesh Upadhyaya, Godampatti, village Shahabpur, 8 February 2003.
7. Pyarelal, interviewed by Sailesh Upadhyaya, Godampatti, village Shahabpur, 8 February 2003.
8. Jhuria, interviewed by Sailesh Upadhyaya, Godampatti, village Shahabpur, 8 February 2003.
9. Bhullar, interviewed by Sailesh Upadhyaya, Godampatti, village Shahabpur, 8 February 2003.
10. Bhullar, interviewed by Sailesh Upadhyaya, Godampatti, village Shahabpur, 8 February 2003.
11. Bhullar, interviewed by Sailesh Upadhyaya, Godampatti, village Shahabpur, 8 February 2003.
12. Khichrilal, interviewed by Sailesh Upadhyaya, Godampatti, village Shahabpur, 8 February 2003.
13. *Hindi Republican Bharat*, 8 May 1968.
14. Quoted in *Shiyo Raj Singh Baichain Hindi Ki Dalit Patrakarita Par Patrakar Ambedkar Ka Prabhav*, Delhi: Samata Prakashan, p. 52.

5

With History and Without History

Dalit Reinvention of the Past*

In this chapter we will examine how the demarginalization of dalits in India works on a variety of levels. Through creating new narratives and virtually inventing a new alternative history and language, this movement, which reached its peak in the decade of the 1980s and 1990s with the formation and growth of the BSP by Kanshiram, used a particular style of popular and widely circulated booklets that were vigorously read and disseminated by the neo-literate dalit population. The construction of this alternative history through such new texts, seen as an existential necessity for the Dalits, worked by weaving together stories found in religious Brahminical popular texts about dissenting lower caste characters, glorified as Dalit heroes who fought against upper caste oppression and injustice. It also included stories of unsung

* This chapter was originally published as an article, 'Demarginalisation and History: Dalit Re-Invention of the Past', in *South Asia Research*, 28(2): 169–84, New Delhi: Sage Publications, July 2008. Copyright © 2008 SAGE Publications. All rights reserved. Reproduced with the permission of the copyright holders and the publishers Sage Publications India Pvt. Ltd, New Delhi.

Dalit freedom fighters, transformed into local myths. Importantly, the language used was different from Standard Hindi, since folk proverbs, idioms and symbols, as well as the grammar and vocabulary of local dialects, were used. However these processes of constructing new history and culture helped only a few dalit castes like the Chamar and the Pasi and to some extent the Dhobi, Khatik, and Balmiki, to become politically empowered and grab an important place in the political domain of India while smaller dalit castes like Sapera, Nat, Musahar, and so on, have not been able to assert for themselves a political space as they do not have an educated and intellectual section to write their caste histories and make their castes visible. As a result these castes have remained marginalized among the entire dalit community and are still languishing on the fringes of the dalits. In this chapter we will examine how the Chamar and Pasi were successful in demarginalizing themselves through the creation of a new history and becoming a part of the mainstream life of India while the smaller dalit castes who did not follow their path, remained behind.

Towards a Democratization of History

A major project of reinventing their own histories took place among a few Dalit communities of UP and Bihar in north India in the decade of the 1980s and 1990s, as we have noted. These histories and new narratives helped these Dalit castes like the Chamar and Pasi to demarginalize themselves and become a part of mainstream contemporary Indian life, while strengthening their own identities, inculcating self-confidence, improving their present, and carving out a brighter future for themselves and their children. Through the exercise of their historical imagination these dalit castes envisioned an alternative past, different from the Brahminical notions of history in which Dalits are presented as degraded social beings and relegated to the fringes of society due to their 'low birth' and certain caste-based 'unclean' occupations.

An exploration of the discursive strategies and politics of imagination and narration of the Dalits' own history is helpful in understanding their protests and demands.[1] This goes much deeper than studying politics, though political parties, especially the BSP, have been using these strategies for mobilizing grassroots Dalits, helping them to demand social, economic, and political privileges based on the history of the injustice done to them. This complex process of identity reconstruction has a deliberately subversive input in socio-political discourses, providing a strong basis for alternative claims that undermine and challenge the historically grown dominant discourses and combat the everyday humiliation still encountered through largely Brahminical and Sanskritic cultural narratives.

This study offers an analysis of the past as an important constitutive element of the recent assertion of a positive Dalit identity and its creative utilization as a liberationist medium for coping with a still oppressive present. An epistemological challenge is made through the creation of history in popular form by booklets and prints composed by the Dalits themselves, together with political discourses of Dalit activists and leaders belonging to literate sections of Dalit communities. From both activities it seems clear that history is being created and epistemologically confronted for direct political purposes.

Over the last two decades, Indian electoral processes and policies of affirmative action have produced some powerful leaders from the Dalit and low-caste communities who have emerged at many different levels of public and political life. The direct impact of this development has been seen in the politics of the historiography of India, an impact that has led to the deconstruction of the legitimacy of history as a disciplined form of knowledge and, as an unavoidable result, its dominant methodologies. The effect of this has been the democratization of history as knowledge of the communities themselves, which ultimately has led to the bigger question of the democratization of history as a discipline. Dalits now claim ownership of historical knowledge about themselves and assert their own interpretations of such knowledge and material.

The recent period has also seen vociferous demands by the marginalized communities for an appropriate share in the power structures of state and society. The past is being openly used—some might argue abused—by these communities to strengthen their demands. To fulfil the need for a past to suit their purpose, the social and historical meaning of the Dalit past is being re-created and reinvented. In this process, the past is intrinsically built into the present; it becomes the subject of present reflection and re-construction as a primary mechanism for changing the marginalized social position of Dalits. Thus their past is one that helps in their ongoing struggle of carving out their future against an oppressive present, constructing an identity that grants them the self-respect to elevate themselves above their present still largely socially degraded status. By rallying around this newly carved positive identity, Dalits and other groups have been politically mobilized in Indian society, bringing about a noticeable change in the socio-political milieu of Indian democracy. Conversely, the changing nature of Indian democracy has also acted as a catalyst for this process.

The power of writing histories is being used by the Dalits as a critique of the nation state through invented narratives of nationalism. These narratives are being generated as a knowledge and resource base for their democratic struggle for a better quality of life. The earlier professional empirical–analytical history, in which Dalits were treated as passive subjects, marginalized them politically and culturally. It made them uninterested, not merely in this kind of history and its concept of truth, but ultimately dispossessed them of the images of their own histories of life in which they have always lived (Turner 1990: 4). Interestingly, this professional history formed the images and representations that intertwined in their memory and myth and served as a vehicle for a more critically informed awareness of the present, to anticipate a future in which they will return to their glorious past. This phenomenon can be widely observed in states like UP, Bihar, and Maharashtra, and is also a growing tendency in Madhya Pradesh, Delhi, and Haryana.

(Hi)Stories of Their Own

The narrative histories (stories or *kathās*) invented by the Dalits constitute an alternative history and language, much of it oral. They tell of Dalit aspirations, dreams, and ambitions and are intended to create more coherent identities among the groups and communities making up this community. The term *kathā* is different from both 'history' as established by Western(ized) academic historians and *itihās* (history) as defined by Indian traditionalist historians as a peculiarly Indian way to know the past through the dominant *Pauranic* tradition of ancient religious texts of the Hindus. Rather, the 'story' or the kathā is a form of liberation for marginalized groups of Indian society that enables them to enter the domain of knowing, inventing, creating, and telling the past (including their own past) as a constant dialogue with the present. The 'story' as narrated by the communities is not just fiction, but is an existential act that reflects living cultural contexts. Various Dalit castes have their own caste stories (*jāti kathā*), written versions of their oral traditions. These stories attempt to represent the traditional or fictional as well as historical past of a particular community and they contain most of the features of narrativity of the oral culture. These *jāti kathā*s are now being claimed as their *jatīya itihās* (caste history), as an expression of subaltern self-consciousness.

This recent assertiveness among lower caste communities in northern India cannot be understood exclusively in terms of their self-definition, but must be seen within the framework of attempts to acquire social respect through such processes. The firm belief that as Dalits they were never provided with what they see as their proper status in Indian historiography has led Dalits to create their own histories. The authors of these histories believe that till now Indian history was mostly written by Brahmin historians, as a result of which the Dalits have not attained the cultural status due to them (Prashant 1994: 3). Thus, history written by Dalits can be called 'Dalit popular history', or a 'people's history of Dalits'. One may also legitimately call it the 'mythistory' of Dalits.

These reinvented histories are circulated within their own community not only through oral culture, but are extended to written tracts in the form of popular booklets printed on cheap newsprint (*akhbāri*) paper and are about 50 to 60 pages in length. Generally, the printing standards are low in Western terms, the form reflecting the lack of money available for their production. However, their content and affordability help to sell them in large numbers in local fairs, meetings, and political rallies. During the last 10 years they have been written and published on a large scale, giving rise to a distinct class of authors and publishers. Many small bookstalls run by Dalit writers can be seen at Dalit political meetings, fairs, and *Chetna Mandap*s, small bookstores set up by the Dalits in district towns and cities to sell books, cassettes and artefacts connected with the Dalit movement. Most of the books deal with Dalit history and literature, while others are biographies and autobiographies of pioneer leaders of the Dalit movement. These Dalit booklets are also displayed along with folk literature in stalls in political fairs.

The newly emerging educated and politically conscious middle stratum of Dalit–Bahujan origin in north India is playing a leading role in writing, publishing, and propagating this kind of Dalit history among the masses. This section was in part built up by Christian missionaries in the eighteenth century who began the process of imparting modern education to the Dalits. The British eventually made education a state subject and invited children from all sections of native society to join schools. Later the Arya Samaj, a prominent Hindu social reform movement started in north India towards the end of the nineteenth century, opened schools for Dalit children and tried to uplift the Dalits under the Brahminical fold by granting them the right to use Brahminical symbols otherwise denied to them by Hindu upper-caste cultural norms. Some Congress leaders and a few philanthropic organizations also opened schools for Dalits in various parts of north India.

In UP, an important social reformer who contributed much to awaken the Dalits was the aptly named Swami Achhootananda,[2] who himself belonged to a Dalit community (Kumar and Sinha 2001: 42). He became a member of the Arya Samaj and played a leading role in raising Dalit literacy levels by setting up a number of schools for Dalit children. He was also a pioneer in inculcating print culture among Dalits, establishing printing presses for publishing Dalit newspapers, books and magazines, and helping to develop an educated and articulate element in Dalit society.

Today this educated and politically conscious middle stratum of Dalit–Bahujan society is active in writing, publishing, and propagating literature related to the Dalit–Bahujan mission of raising the awareness level of the Dalit masses. Analysis of the composition of the BSP shows that it includes 1,20,000 Dalit employees, of whom 500 hold doctoral degrees, 3,000 are doctors, 15,000 are scientists, and 7,000 are graduates (Singh 1994: 88). The steady growth of communication technology, and the use of it by Dalits to write and publish their own popular booklets and pamphlets to propagate their ideas of social justice and equality accelerated the process of undermining prejudice against them throughout the past century, particularly during recent decades. Factors like the development of rapid transportation, growth of modern markets, decline of rural handicrafts and artisanal professions, decrease in the scope of caste-based professions to absorb new entrants, with consequent increases in poverty, and natural calamities that particularly affect poor people, led to the steady migration of many Dalits to urban areas. This exposed them to new life patterns and increased their aspirations for a better future. In addition, their introduction to the politics of identity and self-respect made them ever more conscious of caste hierarchy, giving rise to an urge to challenge and break it. All these factors led to an increase in the reading and writing of booklets centring on history.

The histories written by the Dalits themselves are different from the books authored by professional historians (such as Illaiah 1996; Omvedt 1996) on Dalit history. They are also different from the Dalit history written during the Dalit movement in Maharashtra in the 1960s, in both form and content. These histories also differ from the history of the Shudra castes belonging to the lowest rung of the Hindu caste hierarchy, written by empirical–analytical Marxist historians who attempted to locate that group within a class framework (see Jha 1998). In the Marxist histories of the lower castes, social and economic dimensions are highlighted. However, in Dalit popular history, there is greater emphasis on reconstructing a counter-sociocultural history. The history of Dalits and Bahujans written in UP and Bihar (Prashant 1994; Sagar 1987; Saran 1998), interprets Indian social history through a caste prism in an effective but apparently crude 'story telling' manner.

Dalit Politics and Discourses in North India

The Dalit movement in north India gathered momentum from the end of the nineteenth century and the beginning of the twentieth, although it had strong historical roots. As far back as the medieval period, the *bhakti* movement led by Kabir, Sant Ravidas, and Mirabai contributed a great deal to imparting consciousness of Dalit identity. These poets tried to express pain, pathos, and suffering in a society dominated by Brahminical norms through devotional songs and poetry. Under the influence of some of their leaders, religious groups like the Kabir Panth, Satnami Panth, and the Ravidasi sect were formed. The Arya Samaj also tried to inculcate self-respect in the Dalits, combined with a desire to rise in the social hierarchy by annexing symbols of Brahminical traditions. Their efforts were to integrate the Dalits in respectable Brahminical society by granting them the right to use the symbols denied to them by Hindu Brahminical cultural norms. Though this was actually strengthening the Hindu hierarchic caste-based socio-cultural system, it also provided a kind of feeling of respectable identity to the Dalit communities.

The Adi movement, launched in many parts of the country around the same time and in competition with Christianity (Jenkins 2003), strongly influenced the Dalit movement in north India. This was an assertion of Dalit autonomy within and from Hinduism and the dominant socio-political organizations of upper-caste Hindus. It was led by politicized social activists who claimed that the Dalits and Adivasis were the original inhabitants of this land, enslaved by the conquering Aryans who had come in from Central Asia (Kumar and Sinha 2001: 3). In the later period of his life, Swami Achhootananda left the Arya Samaj to join the Adi movement and worked hard to popularize it in UP.

In south India, there developed a strong Dravidian movement that interpreted history by asserting that in the centuries just before the Christian era, there had been a casteless Tamil culture in south India before the Aryan culture arrived. Early anti-Brahmin parties included the Justice Party founded in 1916, the Self-Respect Movement founded in 1925, and the Dravidian Kazhagam founded in 1944 (Kolenda 1978: 120). Another stream of Dalit reform movements during this period demonstrated the trend towards integration within the existing Hindu social order. Some benevolent Christian missionaries and Muslims, magnanimous Hindus and revolutionary non-Hindus also lent their support to this cause. The

coming of the British exposed these leaders to new values of equality, liberty, and fraternity, given fresh impetus by modern education
and the emergence of new professions (Kumar and Sinha 2001: 3).
The echoes of these movements in south India can be found in one
form or another also in the construction of Dalit consciousness in
north India.

However, the one person who almost single-handedly carved
a new history in the struggle for ameliorating the condition of
the Dalits and raising their socio-political consciousness was Dr
Bhimrao Ambedkar, who started the Dalit movement from the
middle of the second decade of the twentieth century. In the initial
phase of Ambedkar's leadership, his major emphasis was on social
reforms among the Dalits, particularly the untouchable Mahars
of Maharashtra, within the Hindu social order. Later, he sought
political safeguards for all Dalits by asking for Dalit representation
by their own elected leaders. He opposed the 'concession' given to
Dalits through their representatives being nominated by the government, instead of allowing them to elect their own members to
the Council and the Central Legislature. He was also critical of the
philanthropic roles played by the Hindu social reformers and the lip
service extended by the Indian National Congress to the moderate
social uplift of the Dalits. In 1932 he asked for separate electorates
for Dalits, but faced stiff opposition from Mahatma Gandhi who
accepted them for Muslims, Christians, Sikhs, and Anglo-Indians
but, in his commitment to the unity of the Hindu community, drew
the line when it came to untouchables, whose interests he claimed to
represent (Dirks 2001: 269).

After the death of Dr Ambedkar in 1956, the Dalit movement
in UP was taken over by the Agra branch of the RPI, established
in 1958 as the successor of the Scheduled Caste Federation. The
Scheduled Caste Federation of Agra, formed in 1944–5, had been
linked with Dr Ambedkar's All-India Scheduled Castes Federation.

The RPI, which was in contact with branches of the party working in Maharashtra, emphasized the economic, political, and social plight of the Dalits in UP. In 1962, the Agra branch of the RPI contested the general parliamentary elections, winning one seat each for a Member of Parliament and a Member of the Legislative Assembly. But then this independent organization lost in the 1967 general elections and the 1969 mid-term state Assembly elections, and was disbanded in 1969.

After this, the Dalit leadership in the 1970s fell to the Dalit leaders of the Congress Party. Despite the Congress politics of patronage to Dalits, there was insignificant improvement in their general socio-economic status. Indeed, during the 1970s there was a spurt of atrocities on Dalits, which gave birth to the militant Dalit Panther Movement in 1980 in Lucknow and Kanpur, based on the Dalit Panther Movement formed in western India in the 1960s.

With the emergence of the Backward and Minority Communities Employees Federation (BAMCEF) in 1979 in Lucknow, headed by Kanshiram, the Dalit Panther Movement gradually faded out. In 1981, he formed another organization called DS4 (Dalit Soshit Samaj Sangharsh Samiti), a broad-based socio-political platform. In 1984, he launched the BSP on Ambedkar's birth anniversary. This was a full-fledged political party, which fought the general elections with the support of the Dalits, OBCs, and minorities including Muslims, who were at that time together given the nomenclature of *Bahujan*. Kanshiram argued that the Bahujans, who constitute 85 per cent of the country's population, had been suppressed, oppressed, and exploited by the 15 per cent upper caste population (Kumar and Sinha 2001: 70).

In the Dalit and Bahujan discourses that emerged in the Hindi region of northern India, the past increasingly occupied a central place. When north Indian Dalit politics was taking shape, the implementation of the Mandal Commission Report, a commission formed by the Indian government under the prime ministership of Indira Gandhi to formulate protective discrimination policies for the backward and SCs of India, placed history at the forefront in the debates about reserving a certain fixed number of seats in educational institutions and government offices for SCs and STs. The upper castes strongly opposed the implementation of the Mandal Commission Report, saying that merit—and not caste—should be the guiding principle for acquiring jobs and seats in educational institutions. The Scheduled Castes justified these discriminatory protective policies for Dalits by using the logic of past injustices to them by Brahminical culture and power that had historically deprived them of education and jobs (Kushwaha 1993). At the popular level, during mass agitation and self-immolation by some upper-caste students against the implementation of the Report, many scheduled and backward caste organizations distributed leaflets and booklets and delivered popular speeches highlighting the atrocities committed on them in the past that had led to their remaining backward.

In UP, the BSP, in speeches mobilizing illiterate Dalits who had not read Brahminical texts, gave examples showing the ill-treatment of Dalits in ancient Hindu texts, especially in the *Manusmriti*, a *dharmashastra* text attributed to an ancient Indian saint, Manu. The *Manusmriti* is believed to be an ancient Brahminical code of conduct, still followed consciously or unconsciously by most upper-caste Hindus. The essence of *Manusmriti*, also called *Manuvād* by the Dalits, was that Dalits and women, the latter as a category irrespective of their caste, should not have access to wealth, education, and sacred knowledge. As restitution for these historical injustices the party demanded further reparations in the form of reservation or positive discrimination in educational institutions and jobs. Thus the historical debate on ancient Indian society constituted a major plank in the BSP's political discourse (Singh 1994: 13).

Confronting Brahminical History and the Politics of the Past

Dalit history developed in the form of a counter-dialogue against this 'Hindu' history, which continues to play a hegemonic role in Indian social and intellectual life. This history is often presented in the form of *Itihās Purān*, the history that originated from the Pauranic Brahminical texts, circulated circulated widely through rituals, story tellings, religious songs (*kīrtan*s), and in other cultural forms prevalent in everyday life in villages. In these *Itihās Purān*-based cultural performances and discourses, Dalits always find themselves assigned a lower, degraded and 'identity-less' image. As a reaction to this everyday humiliation, the dominant texts of the 'great tradition' and the grand history of the elite were explored meticulously to reject them and offer alternative historical symbols. Epics, scriptures, and ancient religious texts like the *Veda*s, the *Purāna*s, the *Rāmāyana* and the *Mahabharata*, popular among the upper castes in north India, were partially replaced and vigorously contested by folk histories filled with local Dalit heroes. The dominant symbols enshrined in the traditional religious epics were thus challenged, saying that they were full of falsehoods and fiction, used to maintain the intellectual, economic, and cultural superiority of the upper castes.

For example, in discussions on the *Rāmāyana*, Dalits will mention the name of Shambuk, a low-caste character killed by Lord Rama, the upper-caste hero in this epic, for trying to read the *Veda*s. In the story of the *Rāmāyana*, Lord Rama's army, which helped him to rescue his wife, was a motley crowd of monkeys, lower castes, and tribal communities. The Dalits, however, interpret the story as one of injustice against their community, since Lord Rama killed Shambuk, who they claim belonged to a lower caste (Prashant 1994: 16–20). Kanshiram, in one of his speeches for mobilizing Dalits, appealed to them to perform plays based on the life of Shambuk, called *Shambuklīlā*, in place of the *Rāmlīlā*, a popular dramatic performance produced by the upper castes during the Hindu festival of Dussehra (Kushwaha 1996: 11). Similarly, while talking about the *Mahabharata*, Dalits prominently emphasize the injustice done to Eklavya, a low-caste boy who was not accepted as a pupil of the teacher of the rulers because of his caste status. Exploring these intellectual spaces, Dalits develop alternative narratives to counter the 'dominant narrative'. For example, they claim that the composer of the original *Rāmāyana*, Saint Balmiki, came from a lower caste, but is on a par with Tulsidas, the Brahmin saint-poet of the medieval period, who composed *Rāmcharitmānas*, the Brahminical popular version of the *Rāmāyana*.

The task of deconstructing Dalit identity within Brahminical hierarchical parameters was made more arduous because of the various socio-cultural Hindu reform movements that also tried to define Dalit identity. The Arya Samaj Movement and the campaigns by Mahatma Gandhi, who tried to uproot untouchability by giving Dalits the name Harijan, were attempts to create and retain their identity *within* the dominant culture. These imposed identities, however, were not accepted by the Dalits. Mahatma Gandhi, too, who occupies a sacred place in the psyche of the upper castes, was rejected because he wanted to preserve and maintain the hierarchical structure of Indian society by saying that each caste should follow its own caste-based occupation as indicated in the Hindu religious texts. Political efforts to define them in the Marxist paradigm were also strongly rejected. The Dalits wanted to construct their identity by reviving their own folk memories as guided by their contemporary aspirations. Often this process has provided the space for protesting, resisting, and contesting the present structures and also for deconstructing the dominant and hegemonic structures of the past.

The past thus becomes the constitutive element in this exercise of identity construction by the Dalits. This past is a contested terrain, often selectively remembered and sometimes conveniently forgotten. History, therefore, might no longer be regarded as primarily factual, because the facts about the past may actually be imaginations based on the present (Seneviratne 1997: 5). Accounts of the past are embellished and interpreted through the perspective of present-day ethnic and other group identities, aspirations, values, and interests. Whatever facts are known of the past are intermingled with myth and fantasy, and a new perception is created of a glorious past. Selective remembrance from the cluster of popular memories plays an important role in the process of acquiring power and influence, and the symbols, myths, and legends of popular memories that are re-invented in this process give an effective communicative power to the marginalized (Gordon 1995). The significance of this was well understood by the BSP, which has used it as an effective mobilization technique in parliamentary elections since 1995. Other political groups trying to mobilize Dalit votes also employed folk historical narratives for developing interactive relationships between present identity and past.

For meeting the political requirements of this kind of alternative history, the BSP constituted a research committee during the 1990s, composed of Dalit people of the intellectual class in UP to conduct research on popular historical memories and Dalit heroes. Its task includes collating local caste histories and collecting myths and, on that basis, building up Bahujan Dalit literature. This reveals how local caste myths have now become important to the political history ideologues of Dalit and Bahujan politics in the Hindi-speaking region. The activists of the BSP arrange small gatherings and secret meetings among people of specific castes with caste leaders as chief spokespersons. In their speeches they tell of the 'glorious history' of their caste to promote feelings of self-identity. Slowly a belief is disseminated that the caste reached its present deprived state because of earlier conspiracies of the dominant castes. Discussions on 'local and caste history' are also undertaken in these meetings.

The history being circulated through Dalit popular literature influenced by Bahujan politics is now gradually becoming part of the people's memory. During the initial campaign and the formation of the BSP in 1984, a grand Dalit political discourse was established. After 1990, changes were brought in the political language of the party. Apart from the old symbols and icons of Dalit movements, local traditions, caste histories, and myths came to dominate its hustings. A cultural awakening squad was formed to present this discourse of the past through songs, drama, and poetry to ordinary people, performed just before a political meeting to gather a large crowd to listen to the political discourses to follow. Thus stories, cultural performances, and political discourses are intermingled to create popular narratives for mobilizing Dalits. Strategy makers have finally realized the importance of local roots that—for a political price—enabled common people to understand their own values, know their own realities, understand their own mistakes, and help them to advance and progress (Prashant 1994: 5).

Use of the heroic female figures of Jhalkaribai in the Bundelkhand region and Udadevi in the central region of UP are examples of how local figures and histories are used for political mobilization by the BSP. Jhalkaribai, described as a maidservant of Rani Laxmibai, the Queen of Jhansi, who became a heroine of the 1857 Movement when she led her army to defend the kingdom of Jhansi after it was attacked by the British army, appears now in a novel written by Brindavan Lal Varma (1991 [1951]). Jhalkaribai was adapted and cast as a Dalit heroine of the 1857 Revolt and thereby established as a symbol of the active role of Dalits in the freedom struggle. Her statue has been installed close to Rani Laxmibai's fort in Jhansi, where fairs and gatherings are held annually to commemorate her memory.

Similarly, in the Lucknow region, the history and memory of Udadevi, a brave Pasi lady (*vīranganā*) who was a close associate of Begum Hazrat Mahal (a ruler of Lucknow who fought against the British during the 1857 Revolt), was successfully used by the BSP and the Lok Janshakti Party, the Dalit party led by Ram Vilas Paswan. In the Mokama region of north Bihar, the myth of Chuharmal is used for the identity construction and political mobilization of the Dusadhs, a marginalized community of the region (Narayan 2001: 56). Many more examples can be found to show how history is creatively being used in a growing democratization process, emphasizing important contributions of Dalits to strengthen the mobilization of Dalits in various localities in the continuing struggle for acquiring power.

Forms and Features of Dalit History

Dalits believe that their history has four functions. First, it imparts self-respect. Second, they understand their specific place in society. Third, history is a means to acquire self-confidence and self-esteem. And fourth, it establishes a platform for self-analysis. The literate Dalits who claim their narratives to be history, present its ideas through reason and logic to challenge Brahminical beliefs and values based on Hindu religious codes, and deconstruct the dominant and hegemonic upper-caste history and myths. These, they claim, silence Dalit history or describe it as low (*nīch*), degraded (*adham*), or criminal and uncultured (Baudh 1985: 3).

The histories written by the Dalits are figurative, embellished with stories of their popular folk heroes and lower-caste characters of the Brahminical religious texts who had suffered injustice due to their low birth. The language used is Hindi, but not the Sanskritized Hindi used by urban elite people. The sentence construction and vocabulary are based on local folk dialects, filled with popular folk idioms and proverbs familiar to semi-literate Dalits. Although the language cannot be called literary Hindi, the writers of these Dalit histories are more concerned about reaching out to the people in a communicable language that can express their feelings, anger, and dissent against the prevailing caste system than about literary or grammatical standards and precision. Through their localized language and choice of words,

symbols and communicative strategies, they try to create an alternative language for narrating their own history.

There are several other striking features of Dalit history narratives.
First, they project their freedom fighters as unsung heroes of the
freedom struggle in popular booklets, in souvenirs published during
annual conferences of Dalit caste associations, and in other popular
discourses. Some Dalit castes claim in their histories that many of
their heroes were kings who fought against the Mughals and other
invaders, but lost their kingdom due to the conspiracies of the upper-
caste feudal lords (Thakurs) and the priestly caste (Brahmins). Some
castes like the Bhars and Pasis, now among the lowest castes of Dalits
in north India, describe their role as freedom fighters who laid down
their lives to free the nation from external aggressors (Chaudhary
1997: 16).

Another feature of Dalit story telling is that folk lyrical metres
such as the *doha, chaupai, chaubol,* or *lahara* are widely used to make
the narrative more powerful and communicative. Narrating a peasant
uprising that took place in Tanda, near Faizabad, UP in 1918, called
the *Tanda Kisan Andolan,* the author Pawan (1992: 9) expresses himself in the following poetic metres:

> *Utpidan samrajya is kadar chhaya tha*
> *Babu-retiyon ki izzat bhi nahi surakshit*
> *Goodar Ram us samay atyachar ke virodh mein*
> *Khade ho gaye shakti dhariya man mein kar sanchit.*

The oppressive reign was so pervasive and dominant that the purity
and honour of daughters and daughters-in-law was not safe. At that
time with chivalry and patience Goodar Ram stood up in opposition
to the tyranny of the British.

> *Gaon gaon ja ja kushti aadhaar banaakar*
> *Yuvakon ka sanghathan ek majboot kar liya*

Aur akhade ke agua ko har gaon mein
Krishak sanghathan ka bhar de diya

Youths were invited to practise wrestling in every village and an organization was formed. The leader of the wrestling centre (*akhada*) in
each village was made responsible for peasant organization.

The narrative strategies of their history writing, either based on
historical events of peasant movements during the colonial period, or
caste histories, emerge by searching for and developing myths to support their claims. This is epistemologically different from the rational
or scientific representation of professional or modernist history writing. Dalit history writing uses poetry, a variety of folk metres, and
story telling of an overt political nature. Popular idioms and folk terminology is also widely used. Through various folk stanzas, *chhanda*,
doha, *chaupai*, *dauda*, *ghazal*, *qawwali*, or *chauboli*, poets try to speak
their 'own history'. The tradition of orality remains predominant,
although booklets of historical songs written in these forms and illus-
trated with pictures are sold and purchased in large numbers.

In the process of writing their own history, Dalits have thus
attempted to develop a counter-historical discourse by exploring oral
traditions. Essentially, these alternative histories have tried first to
deconstruct dominant Brahminical epical myths and history; second, to explore history, caste history and narratives glorifying the
local myths of Dalit castes; and third, to record the unwritten history of Dalit leaders, saints, and social reformers. As often noted by
Mayawati, the westernized and educated people who wrote history
wiped out all traces of Dalit kings and emperors, rajas and maharajas.
While important Dalit rulers like Bijli Pasi found no mention in
history books, although there is strong evidence that the Pasis were
once rulers of the region, Mayawati claims that the Dalits are not
inventing history, but are merely highlighting a hidden history, one
that has been consciously suppressed (Chaudhary 1997: 2).

The new Dalit history seems to be not unified but fragmentary in nature. Small episodes narrating incidents of dissent by Dalits found in various locally narrated popular Hindu texts, are woven together to form a grand Dalit history. These include Dalit interpretations of stories like the Shambuk and Eklavya episodes from the *Rāmāyaṇa* and the *Mahabharata*. Sometimes the histories of the various Dalit castes based on folklore may not be uniform, but contesting myths of the same story can be found. For example, in the Mithila region there is a story about Dina Bhadri, a hero of the Musahar caste, a very low caste known to eat rats, and usually employed for ploughing fields. Dina Bhadri was killed by Sahlesh, a hero of the Dusadh caste, a Scheduled Caste known for its martial instincts and for rearing pigs. But in the written form, Dalit historians try to downplay the killing of the hero of one community by a member of a similarly disadvantaged group to avoid confrontation of the two castes. In UP, Dalit historians highlight both Jhalkaribai, of the Kori caste, as well as Udadevi, of the Pasi caste, as heroines of a homogeneous Dalit community. At the same time, the Kori and Pasi castes individually identify Jhalkaribai and Udadevi respectively with their own castes. Thus caste identities are converted in a number of ways into a broad Dalit identity in their written histories to ally all Dalit castes.

Writers of Dalit popular history enter the memories of Dalits in two ways. First, they explore the content and form of their folk memories. Second, they serve as a link between the popular medium and folk memory. Some of these popular historiographers clearly enter into Dalit politics, while others choose to remain outside. In UP, Bahujan politics have caused an increase in the composition and publication of such types of popular history and literature. In the political discourse of Bahujan politics also, local, popular, and Dalit caste histories are used for political mobilization and substantially contribute to the flourishing of such popular history and literature. In Bihar, too, the use of popular myths like that of Chuharmal and

Sahlesh by the Dalit Sena, a branch of the Lok Janshakti Party of Ram Vilas Paswan, clearly reveals this growing trend.

In this chapter we demonstrated that the reinvention and writing of their own histories by the Dalit communities of UP and Bihar in northern India is helping to demarginalize these communities and allows them to acquire a respectable position in contemporary Indian society. In this process, the Dalits are strengthening their own individual and collective identities, acquiring self-confidence, improving their condition and carving out a new future through histories circulated via popular booklets. Such publications are also creatively used for mobilizing grassroots Dalits and their political interests by Bahujan political leaders. This also supports Dalit demands for greater social, economic, and political rights based on the history of injustice done to them in the past. In other movements, the idea of being the original inhabitants of the subcontinent is used as an instrument to motivate the masses to acquire social respect and a better quality of life.

Such developments display an avowedly political character. Two main objectives of the BSP, visible in its historical language, are to develop a homogeneous identity among the fragmented Dalit castes, and to inject and encourage necessary feelings of suspicion and class opposition against the upper castes. The reconstruction of the past provides support for claiming acquisition of more democratic and other benefits today and particularly to justify positive discrimination policies for Dalits. Subverting the dominant discourse provides at the same time a strong basis for an alternative.

The construction of an alternative history for the Dalits combats also the everyday humiliation encountered through dominant Brahminical cultural narratives. It is mainly created by both opposing and weaving together stories in religious Brahminical popular texts about dissenting lower-caste characters. Dalit history glorifies Dalit heroes and heroines who fought against the oppression and injustice of the upper castes and of colonial rule. The stories of unsung Dalit heroes who participated in the freedom struggle and have been transformed into myths in the local oral traditions are central to their history. The language of these histories circulated through popular booklets is necessarily different from standard hindi in their use of folk proverbs, idioms and symbols, as well as grammar and vocabulary.

These new histories are political mechanisms and tools for carving out a better future position of the Dalits. With the growing democratization process and the political need to incorporate marginalized and minority communities, the boundaries of history are expanded beyond the empirical–analytical to include the myths and heroes of the subaltern entrant communities. These new histories may prove to be histories of the future of the Dalits, as well as other marginalized and subaltern communities in South Asian societies that will help to demarginalize them, freeing them from the burdens of the past.

In the next chapter we will delve into the issues of caste identities, their formation, assertion, creation of layers of dominance, exclusion, and marginalization. All these present a complex scenario, wherein the ever-changing flux in the socio-political matrix of democracy is a challenge. Not to speak of castes that lost their voice and position due to various factors, even dominant dalit castes like the Chamars have had a very complex relationship among themselves.

Notes

1. Important reading on this is found, among others, in Hoy (1986), Norris (1992), Bhabha (1994), Chakrabarty (2003), and Davies (2003).
2. This name conveys something like 'the pleasure of being untouchable'.

6

Culture and Representation
The Making of Public Culture

This chapter shows how the attempts to reconstruct a form of public culture through intervention by the Indian state in the 1980s saw the establishment of seven Zonal Cultural Centres (ZCCs) in different parts of the country. The chapter examines how these ZCCs ignored the art and culture of marginalized Dalit castes of UP, thus defeating their very purpose, which was to provide space to all communities of the country and promote a 'people's culture'. The decade of the 1980s in India was marked by a serious crisis in the country, and the challenge before Rajiv Gandhi, the then prime minister, was to create a national culture in a step towards rebuilding the nation and also to reinforce the identities of migrants thronging urban areas in India and abroad in search of employment. He did this by setting up the ZCCs, since culture is an important tool of the state not only to contain 'national crisis' but also to justify the state's legitimacy as part of nation-building. In this chapter, through a detailed study of the ZCCs and a field study of the North Central ZCC in Allahabad, we will analyse how these centres only catered to the demands of the market economy by promoting a few colourful, vibrant cultural forms of select states that came to symbolize Indian culture all over the world, and neglected cultural forms like Pasiawa, Ahirwa, Chamaraundha and others specific to Dalit castes of UP (see Figure 6.1).

For marginalized communities like the Dalits and lower castes, the desire to acquire power is strongly linked with the transformation of their various kinds of invisibilities into visibilities, enabling them to fulfil their desire to gain representation in history, culture, and the public space. This process can be observed in UP where, besides seeking to enhance their political power, the Dalits of this state are also trying to gain representation in these spheres. The fulfilment of their desire to gain representation in history can be seen in the surge since the 1960s in the production of numerous Dalit popular booklets that highlight the contribution of Dalits in India's history. The desire for visibility in public space in towns, cities, and

Figure 6.1 Chamaraundha Dance Performance at Jaunpur District, Uttar Pradesh, India
Source: Brijendra Gautam.

districts is being fulfilled by installing statues of Dalit heroes and building parks in their name, while their representation in public culture is seen in the revival of their traditional folk songs and dances. Interestingly, the Dalit communities of UP had rejected their cultural traditions between 1950 and 1980 as they developed a new feeling of self-respect, causing them to perceive these cultural forms as symbols of their humiliation. In the last century the Chamars of UP had also undertaken a social movement to discontinue their caste-based profession of skinning and tanning dead cattle and cutting of the umbilical cord. They had also stopped performing their traditional dance, called *Chamarachna*, because viewers from the upper- and middle- castes used to taunt them for these symbols of their caste identity. At that time these cultural forms had become a cultural space where they repeatedly experienced humiliation.

However, now that the Dalits have gained political power in UP, the people of the Chamar community living in various parts of the state are once again keen to revive these cultural forms as symbols of their self-respect and caste identity in order to acquire representation in public culture as well. For example, the Chamar residents of village Kajishahpur, Khutahan in Jaunpur district in north India, are keen to revive the folk dance they had rejected many years ago, and for this they are trying to enlist the help of the government. Dalit intellectuals of Allahabad, such as Guru Prasad Madan, feel that the government should form a cultural policy through which the caste-based culture of the Dalits is revived, while the Dalit Cultural Association of Azamgarh is constantly demanding that Dalit cultural forms be given importance in the cultural policies of the government. However, if one studies the history of the agenda of the government's cultural policies, one finds that there is minimal space for the culture of the Dalits. In order to study this process it is important to see how the state has perceived culture in its policies and to analyse the direction of the formation of its cultural policies.

Cultural Politics and Formation of the ZCCs

As we have seen, the ZCCs were cultural institutions set up by the Ministry of Human Resources Development under the Department of Culture, Government of India, in the mid-1980s to preserve, promote, and disseminate the composite culture of the nation. They were envisaged to include all the cultures of the country, including marginalized and vanishing art forms, and thereby present a mosaic of unity in diversity. Seven ZCCs were set up, covering the entire nation. Several states were part of more than one ZCC, as per policy decision. The North Zone Cultural Centre (NZCC) was situated at Patiala. The members were Jammu and Kashmir, Himachal Pradesh, Punjab, Haryana, Chandigarh, and Rajasthan. The North Central Zone Cultural Centre (NCZCC) was situated at Allahabad. The member states were Madhya Pradesh, Rajasthan, Haryana, Bihar, UP, and Delhi. The Eastern Zone Cultural Centre (EZCC) was situated at Kolkata. The members were Bihar, West Bengal, Orissa, Assam, Tripura, Manipur, Sikkim, and the Union Territory of Andaman and Nicobar Islands. The North East Zone Cultural Centre (NEZCC) was situated at Dimapur. The member states were Assam, Tripura, Manipur, Arunachal Pradesh, Nagaland, and Meghalaya. The South Zone Cultural Centre (SZCC) was situated at Thanjavur. The members were Kerala, Tamil Nadu, Andhra Pradesh, Karnataka, Union Territory of Andaman and Nicobar Islands, Lakshadweep, and Pondicherry. The South Central Zone Cultural Centre (SCZCC) was situated at Nagpur. The member states were Madhya Pradesh, Maharashtra, Karnataka, and Andhra Pradesh. The West Zone Cultural Centre (WZCC) was situated at Udaipur. The members were Goa, Gujarat, Rajasthan, Maharashtra, and the Union Territory of Daman, Diu, and Dadra and Nagar Haveli.

The ZCCs were created in the mid-1980s with the deliberate aim of combating the political crisis then confronting India: the turmoil in Punjab and the consequent deaths of thousands in the wake of terrorism, the attack on the Golden Temple 'to flush out terrorism and extremism from Punjab', then prime minister Indira Gandhi's assassination and the large-scale anti-Sikh riots that followed. In fact, the report of the High Powered Committee set up in 1994–5 by the Ministry of Human Resource Development to review the seven ZCCs (hereinafter 'Report') also states that 'the idea of setting up the ZCCs occurred at the time of a national crisis' (Government of India 1994–5: 8). The situation in Punjab led the then prime minister Rajiv Gandhi to formally announce the setting up of the ZCCs at Hussainiwala in Punjab on 23 March 1985 while laying the foundation stone of the Bhagat Singh Memorial. Rajiv Gandhi announced this during a serious, concerned speech about Punjab's political and economic crisis. The Report records Rajiv Gandhi as saying

> Culture has also suffered a great deal in the past years. It is our desire to see that culture gets a boost in Punjab and it looks to the future. Towards this end, we will set up a Zonal Cultural Centre for the … Northern zone in the state. We will ensure that *the centre nurtures and helps to further the culture* [italics for emphasis] not only of the state but whole of northern India. (Report 1994–5: 5)

The choice of place and the occasion where the formation of the ZCCs was announced was of significance in shaping their laudable objective of forming a national culture that would be inclusive and expansive besides making the people of Punjab feel that they were a part of the composite culture of India. It is important to note that the then prime minister regarded national unity and integration as among the most important means of pursuing the agenda of nation-building and used culture towards achieving this end. Through the ZCCs, the Indian government was trying to make national culture homogeneous so as to manage regional and ethnic contestations in Indian society. It was trying to develop a national culture that was a convergence of diverse cultural forms, ethos, and lives. The idea of using culture in the project of nation-building was also reflected in the structure of the ZCCs as conceptualized by the GoI. The government devised a three-tier system of control, comprising the ZCC members, the Zones, and the Centre (the Union Government). It was believed that the separate identities of the members as well as their cultural kinship as revealed by their various arts and cultural forms would be showcased through this system, and that, in this way, the ZCCs would be 'highlighting unity in diversity of the Indian heritage' (Report 1994–5: 6).

The use of terms like 'protect', 'preserve', 'disseminate', and 'nurture' in the context of national culture showed that the ZCCs were envisioned as the 'guardians' and 'custodians' of national culture, thus underlining their patronizing attitude towards culture. This attitude is also visible in the annual report of the Ministry of Culture (2007–8), which mentioned that their mandate was to 'preserve and promote all forms of art and culture'. In the discussion regarding the formation of the cultural centres, ideas like 'ensuring the role of culture in nation building', 'fusing of numerous cultures into composite culture', and 'instrument of social change to bring about national integration' are mentioned, revealing the actual intent of these centres. Since their chief function lies in selecting nationalist elements from people's culture that may be helpful in governance and the nation-building project, the centres are the 'production units of national culture' with the state determining how 'national culture' is defined. This shows that the government perceives culture as an important instrument in the project of nation-building and transforming people into 'national subjects'. In the process the state also acquires the justification to govern culture in the name of nation-building.

Even now the Indian government is thinking of forming a national policy on culture. In October 2006 a committee was constituted by the Culture Ministry asking its members to frame a 'national culture'.

The committee featured 19 eminent personalities such as Professor U.R. Ananthamurthy, Girish Karnad, Shyam Benegal, M.T. Vasudevan Nair, Professor Mushirul Hasan, Mallika Sarabhai, Ashok Vajpeyi, and Ramachandra Guha. It was asked to study the extent and role of government in various areas of culture and also to assess the mandate for various cultural institutions (Sinha 2007). However, what the government and state overlooks in the pursuit of its agenda for using culture towards nation-building is that many marginalized and dying cultures are ignored. In the use of culture in the politics of nation-building, a process of internal colonialism occurs in the form of marginalization and suppression of minorities and indigenous people that hurts the making of cultural democracy (Pieterse 2004: 63). It reduces culture to an instrument in the nation-building process and transports it to a state-managed domain. In this process, the autonomy of culture as a creative domain is diluted.

State, Market, and Culture

Alongside the political turmoil of the 1980s India, an economic turmoil had also been activated as the ground was prepared for a new economic policy, formally implemented in the 1990s. Indian society had started gearing up to face the changes set in motion all over the world by the forces of globalization. The advent of computers and other modern technology also led to changes in society as new avenues of employment opened up. The middle class had more money at its disposal and the demand for material comforts prompted by the bazaar and advertisements started increasing. New economic terms were creeping into the vocabulary of the people and middle-class aspirations started growing. There was also a sharp increase in migration to urban areas as more and more people from villages and small towns moved to big cities. This caused a great upheaval in society, since the process of uprooting themselves from their native place invariably triggered a sense of alienation despite the increased material comforts.

Using culture to combat the sense of alienation in migrants was another motive behind the ZCCs mooted by Rajiv Gandhi. Believing that mass migration from the villages was leading to the creation of a new kind of urban space, cultural institutions were asked to organize cultural events like *Apna Utsav* (Our Festival) in urban areas which included folk performances from different parts of the country to soothe the gnawing alienation in the migrant population. This is clear in the Report:

> For the first time, millions were (and are) leaving their homes and going to different areas looking for occupations other than tradition-ally what has been their familial occupation and, in doing this, creat-ing a tremendous geographic uprooting of our society. In the past, only those who joined the army or had business interests went to the other parts of the country. Mass movement is now the domi-nant factor which contributes to the fast pace of economic devel-opment. When people leave their villages for want of facilities and amenities and go to urban areas they get cut off from their traditional culture and are faced in this new environment with a breakdown of their traditional values, snapping of links with the old culture. It is this churning, this *manthan* (churn, swirl) that causes many of the problems in our society today. Millions are now living and working with people of different castes and communities, different linguis-tic groups, people of different regions, a countrywide mixing of this diversity and knowledge has come about but people tend to go back to their language, their culture, and their religion as a support. So the challenge to national integration is in preventing this great movement that is taking place from becoming a platform for individual rivalries, community rivalries or linguistic rivalries. (Report 1994–5: 57)

An interesting point in the context of cultural governance by the state is that as the market, which was earlier under the control of the state, started liberating itself and its tentacles began spreading, it also began making inroads into the state mechanism governing culture. Slowly but surely the terms and language of the market and management started finding expression in state governance. Concepts like 'association of production units' and 'distribution network', which essentially belong to the market, also began to be used in relation to the formation of the ZCCs. This was evident in the speeches of Mani Shankar Aiyar, a bureaucrat then and politician now, who played a pivotal role in the formation of the ZCCs. He used the marketing language and also compared the distribution network of culture with that of ITC's distribution network for cigarettes. He stated,

> The ZCCs were conceived as distribution networks. However when Rajiv Gandhi had to decide how much money would have to be given to these centres, the truth dawned on him (which anybody who works for a commercial structure knows) that for mass produced goods the largest investment has to be in the distribution infrastructure. ITC, for example, and I mention this deliberately, invests much less in farms and factories than it does in distribution because cigarettes have to be made available in every village of India. Therefore, if we have a distribution network for Indian culture, we should have a reach at least as big as the ITC reach for cigarettes. This was not appreciated as a starved and deprived but hoary cultural network. But the capital expenditure came from the budget of India. (Report 1994–5: 58)

In conjunction with aiming to bring about a cultural unification of the country, catering to the needs of the market was another objective of the government, and so its cultural policies gave importance to the visual arts or the visual aspects of the performing arts. The logistics of marketing and advertisement too are based on the visual aspect and therefore the ZCCs became more of a state project to create a cultural market that focused on visual aspects of the performing arts that could be made into consumable 'national culture' for the growing middle class in urban areas. In other words, the new cultural centres played a pivotal role in commodifying exotic and awe-inspiring performing arts that could amaze urban dwellers. In other words, 'the other' cultures such as the tribal, folk, and ethnic cultures that could satiate the alienated and rootless urban population and connect them with their roots were given top priority. Thus, the post-1984 cultural promotion by the state comfortably adapted to market idioms and culture to establish harmony between the state and culture. This was totally antithetical to the earlier state promotion of composite culture through literary production, and promotion of handloom industries, which were to stand for national culture.

However, although visual culture was given precedence over literary arts, only a small number of folk cultural forms from a few states like Gujarat, Rajasthan, Punjab, Madhya Pradesh, and so on, were selected for nurturing and fostering. These forms included Pandvani, a folk cultural form of Madhya Pradesh, Ghoomar, a folk dance of Rajasthan, Bhangra, the folk dance of Punjab, Garba, a folk dance of Gujarat, and some folk dance and music from Himachal Pradesh, all of which had the dancers and singers wearing colourful and exotic costumes. These could be easily marketed worldwide because of their visual appeal, and were prominently highlighted by the ZCCs. The artistes who performed these folk dances were also those with the ability, through their aggressive marketing skills, to impress the selection experts authorized by the government. These artistes were then taken under the wings of government officials and bureaucrats responsible for governing culture, and their careers skyrocketed under state patronage. Each cultural event organized by cultural institutions in different parts of India and abroad, like the festivals of India in Paris, the USA, London, and so on, included these artistes, while other budding and upcoming artistes and other cultural forms were completely marginalized. Notable among these folk artistes whose careers soared due to state patronage was Teejan Bai, a folk singer belonging to a tribe in Madhya Pradesh who became famous for performing the Pandvani—a little-known performing art that eulogized the Pandavas (heroes of the *Mahabharata*). No cultural event organized by cultural institutions was complete without a Pandvani performance by Teejan Bai—even the television channel Doordarshan, run by the Government's Ministry of Information and Broadcasting, would regularly telecast her performances.

This patronage by the government and state has resulted in a kind of internal colonialism in the field of art and culture in which a few cultural forms enjoy hegemony over the rest which remain suppressed and marginalized. Noteworthy among them are the cultural art forms of different Dalit castes of UP like *Pasiawa*, the folk dance of the Pasis; *Chamaraundha*, the folk dance of the Chamars; the *Dhobi naach* of the Dhobis; *Domkuch* of the Dom caste; *Gondnach* of the Gond community in eastern UP and Bihar, and folk dances of other Dalit castes. Apart from these visible dalit and OBC castes there is another level of invisibility among the dalits. These castes include the most marginalized dalit castes like Sapera, Nat, Musahar, Pattharkat, Kanjar, and so on, about whom our state discourse of language cannot even imagine that they have their own cultural forms and that they should be given space in the country's cultural discourse. For example, the Pattharkat caste, which is involved in stone breaking, have a tradition of singing work songs but these have never been recorded or documented or given space in state-supported cultural policies. The Musahars and Nats both have a rich cultural heritage in which they sing and dance during their wedding ceremonies but this heritage has remained invisible to the state cultural administration.

Just as Dalits have historically been exploited by the upper castes for their so-called polluting and demeaning jobs, their culture too has been marginalized by Brahmin socio-cultural norms. The upper-caste people looked down upon their cultural performances as uncouth and vulgar since they were usually performed late at night in the community's hamlets, often with the performers and audience somewhat drunk on country liquor and behaving in a rowdy and boisterous manner. Although these castes exist in Hindu societies all over the country, in most parts of India social movements have liberated them from the traditional polluting caste-based jobs that were the cause of their backward status. Socially and culturally assimilated into the mainstream elsewhere, in UP (India's Hindi heartland and one of its largest and most populated states) these communities remained marginalized in the state's fragmented social fabric because of the continued prevalence of Brahminical socio-cultural norms till recently. It was only after the emergence and rise in UP in the 1980s of the BSP—the political party whose sole ideology is the uplift of the Dalits—that the Dalits of this state became politically empowered. The BSP is one of the most powerful parties in UP. However, the cultural empowerment of the Dalits with their cultural resources as their identity markers has yet to take place since educated Dalits have become highly Sanskritized and have rejected their original caste-based culture while the poor Dalits living in rural areas are still socio-economically marginalized and do not have a voice to assert their cultural heritage despite their political empowerment. In such a situation the cultural resources of the Dalits of UP like the *Pasiawa, Chamaraundha, Ahirwa, Dhobi Naach*, and so on, have been deprived of state patronage through the ZCCs, whose chief objective was the nurturing and fostering of marginalized cultures in order to make them a part of India's national culture.

Culture and the Margins

In order to get a first-hand idea of the cultural policies of the government with respect to the lower castes, we conducted an in-depth study of the NCZCC situated in Allahabad, which is the ZCC responsible for promoting the art and culture of UP. The study was carried out in

December 2009, and we spoke to a few artisans who had come to the Shilp Mela (crafts fair) organized by the NCZCC to display and sell their traditional handicrafts. The Shilp Mela is a 15-day handicrafts fair held on the NCZCC grounds every December. Artisans from different parts of the country display and sell their work and folk artistes, also from different parts of the country, showcase their art and culture in the evenings. From the random survey we found a kind of pattern in which the same set of people are called to either perform or put up stalls every year. This shows a clear lack of research and field study by NCZCC as it did not survey the villages and tribal communities regarding their traditional art and culture and was quite clueless about the artistes, artisans, and cultural forms existing there.

We found that popular artifacts and crafts, which have a demand in the market, had an edge over neglected and vanishing art forms. Furthermore, the same persons had been attending the Shilp Mela for the past several years. For example, Afzal Ahmad from Mubarakpur, Azamgarh, who was selling handloom saris, had been coming to the Shilp Mela for nine years. Sriram Modi from Jhunjhunu district, Rajasthan, who was selling traditional Rajasthani *lehanga-chunri* (the traditional long skirt, top, and a pretty scarf for young girls and women) had been participating for five years. Abdul Rehman from Nawalgarh, Rajasthan, who was manning a traditional painting stall and was representing an NGO called Murarka Foundation, too had been attending the Mela for five years. It was also the fifth year for Jaswinder from Punjab who was selling woollen items made in his state, whereas for Babu Lal Gola, from Faridabad, Haryana, selling attractively painted clay and stone artifacts it was the fourth year. For Afzal of Kashmir who was selling Pashmina shawls, it was the fourth year as well, while for Saquoor Ahmad from Jaipur it was the third year. The only exception was Eklaque Ahmad from Madho Singh, Ghosnia, in Badhoi district, UP, who had come to the Shilp Mela for the first time.

We also found that many middlemen, traders, showrooms, and so on had become a part of the Mela. For example, Sriram Modi from Jhunjhunu district, Rajasthan, belongs to the Bania (trading) community. He procures traditional Rajasthani dresses from the artisans and sells them at fairs like the Shilp Mela in Allahabad. He has been doing this for five years. Similarly, Abdul Rehman, who was selling traditional Rajasthani paintings, represented an NGO. Manoj Srivastava, representing Tribes India, was a Central Government employee selling tribal art and craft on behalf of the government. This was resulting in the further marginalization of the community artisans and craftsmen who should have been participating in the mela independently. Another fact that surfaced was that some stalls at the Mela were auctioned at high prices to the sellers, which was a sharp pointer that NCZCC was more concerned about its profit rather than the welfare of the artisans and craftsmen. Due to the auctioning process, poor craftsmen were being marginalized and deprived of the opportunity of showcasing and selling their wares directly.[1]

In the domain of folk traditions we found that established folk songs like *Kajri*, *Chaiti*, *Aalha*, *Birha*, and *Pandavani* were regularly performed at the fairs and the same artistes were invited again and again to perform. This points to a strong nexus between the small-time artistes and the organizers as most of these artistes were locally based and were often used as fillers in major programmes. The marginalized folk cultures of villages adjoining Allahabad like *Pasiawa*, *Chamaraundha*, *Ahirwa*, and so on were not represented at all at any of the Shilp Melas organized by the NCZCC every year. According to Bhawra, a Pasi folk singer of *Pasiawa*, who is highly regarded by the folk singers of Allahabad, he is never invited to perform at any of the fairs organized by the NCZCC although the organizers are well aware of his reputation in Allahabad and the adjoining areas. He attributes this to the mindset of the organizers who are still under the sway of the Brahminical socio-cultural norms and do not accord a high status to the folk culture of the lower castes.

The report of the high-powered committee appointed by the Ministry of HRD to review the seven ZCCs, bears testimony to our study of the Shilp Mela. The report says:

> It was our impression while we went around the ZCCs that in the field of crafts, textiles and handicrafts, not much research have (sic) taken place to find the genuine practitioners of these arts in the remote corners of the country. In such situations, the temptation is often to invite the same groups, who became experts in participating in Melas. A genuine effort should be made to break the formation of such vested-interest groups and find actual practitioners of these crafts, who may not even be aware of avenues like the ZCCs ... a ZCC Mela, ought not to be merely an outlet for sales. There is a whole way of life, and a vision of life in the practice of these crafts and it is more important that this aspect of crafts should come through as a living alternative to our modern civilization. (Report 1994–5: 13)

The high-powered committee of the ZCCs suggested that more importance be given to the folk forms, which is its avowed policy. It mentions that the ZCCs' *finances and resources could well be utilized by giving life to segments like folk and tribal arts, which no other organization supports* (italics for emphasis) (Report 1994–5: 6).

In our study, we found that the dictates of the market economy continued to promote those art forms which were in demand while many marginal art forms of the Dalits like *Chamaraundha* (dance form of the Chamars) and popular Dalit folk ballads like *Reshma-Chuharmal, Dina-Bhadri, Shobh-Nayaka Banjara, Behula-Lakhandar*, and so on, about caste heroes and love stories of struggle and conflict, are never presented by the NCZCC. There may be two possible reasons for this: first, that these forms do not have a ready market as these are not part of the habitual taste of the masses, and second, that no member of any of the Dalit communities participates in any policy-making body of the NCZCC. Furthermore, except some repertoire of the oral narratives and traditions, the major traditions in Bhojpuri, Maghai, Awadhi, Braj, Bundeli, Maithili, and so on, too do not find space in the scheme of things in the NCZCC. This creates another kind of marginalization of the oral traditions. It is quite evident that the NCZCC is not prepared to take a creative risk and create a space for these marginal oral forms. The high-powered committee's report also states that many of the rich folk art forms are on the verge of extinction because of lack of support and it is only the ZCCs that can save it (Report 1994–5: 11). It was expected that the ZCCs would fill this gap but these cultural institutions, too, fell prey to market forces.

Culture and Audience

For any market to survive, the demand side (audience/target audience) is of paramount importance. In fact, the supply side has to constantly monitor, change, and adapt according to the shifting tastes of its audience(s). Unfortunately, in the context of the ZCCs, both the supply side and the demand side remain vague and nebulous. The lack of understanding of culture by bureaucrats (Government of India 1994–5) and their office is paralleled and mirrored in the audience that comes to attend the functions and fairs. Initially, when the NCZCC in Allahabad was being set up it was mandatory for the office staff to be present during all the functions organized by the centre. When the crowd was thin the staff was made to sit among the audience and applaud with the people. If the audience swelled—as it did for some select programmes like Kathak recital, and so on—this 'fake audience' turned into 'volunteers', sporting the badges hitherto hidden in pockets for bigger events. Friends and family of the office staff too had to attend functions like *Chalo Man Ganga Yamuna Teer* (O Mind! Let's go to the banks of Ganga and Yamuna), during the Magh/Kumbha Mela. There was an almost mad rush among the officers and staffers of the NCZCC to bring in the maximum number of people. It seemed that each of them had become a 'shepherd' in the Christian sense, collecting and exhibiting their 'small flock' to the top bosses. Free food was an incentive, so were free tents (a prize during Kumbha Mela). Hordes of people from the villages of the staffers could be seen on the banks of the Sangam, attending evening events as the audience.

A second category of this 'fake audience' were top bureaucrats—with their wives and children in town—who would come to 'party' in the evenings, with free songs and dances as icing on the cake. These bureaucrats were from the same or adjoining districts, friends, or friends of friends of other bureaucrats. Guests also included top officials from the ministries, where sycophancy was at its best. Officers of the NCZCC focused only on the *khatirdari* (hospitality and appeasing of senior officers) and the actual cultural events were forgotten. At different levels, the effort was to 'please' the boss, or in this case, the boss's boss. It was a perverse and blatant misuse of public funds. A different 'culture', one that helped cultivate powerful people for personal gains, could be seen, and remains to this day.

A third category of audience that emerged over time was the rich, bored with nothing-to-do-at-home women, wives, and kin of rich citizens—bureaucrats, lawyers, businessmen—who lived in the vicinity of NCZCC. Though a shift from 'fake audience' to a 'semi-real audience' began, it was quite clear that this was still not the 'real audience'. For this category, these events were an occasion to meet and gossip. It was an extension of their kitty parties and clubs. They came dolled up, exhibiting their expensive dresses and ornaments.

Thus the ZCCs, which were set up by the state to promote cultural centres, have only continued to promote art forms that would meet the demands of the cultural elite of India. Not only does this marginalize Dalit cultural forms, but there is also a lack of representation of Dalits in high-powered cultural bodies like the zonal centres and this further reduces the focus on and knowledge of Dalit culture at the decision-making level. The cultural politics of the Indian state show that the state has selectively used particular forms of popular culture in its hegemonic project to serve the interest of the privileged groups. The state has attempted to commodify culture to cater to the consumer desires of the urban population. Further, it shows how, compelled by the market economy, culture has been extracted to be merely equated with external forms, symbols and artifacts—such as the idea that local culture could be purchased in melas, and in the process completely marginalized the idea that culture is also about lived experiences and closely linked with issues of citizenship and with the politics of exclusion and inclusion. As all zonal centres are city-centric, mainly catering to the interests of the urban public, the promotion of folk arts through these centres has been artificial rather than vibrant and alive. The zonal centres and their market-oriented melas seem to be marginal to the state's own attempt to use culture towards 'nation building', as these activities are also marginal to the lives of the vast majority of Indian communities who are neither suppliers nor consumers.

As in the domain of politics and society, in the domain of culture too the culture of marginalized dalit castes like Sapera, Bansphor, Pattharkat, Musahar, and so on, have remained marginalized within the culture of the overall dalit culture, which itself is still marginalized and looked down upon by the elite upper castes although the visible and politically powerful dalit castes like the Chamar and Pasi are trying to make their cultural forms more visible. Thus these invisible dalit castes are being denied cultural citizenship in the country and continue to remain suppressed and marginalized in each domain of the society.

Note

1. Interview of the stall owners at NCZCC Shilp Mela, Allahabad, by Nivedita Singh and Brijendra Gautam, dated 24 December 2009.

Conclusion

In this book, I have tried to understand the dilemma and struggle within the entire dalit community of UP for acquiring visibility, empowerment, and political space. In UP the dalits together comprise 21 per cent of the total population of the state and comprise nearly 66 castes. Of this the Chamars make up the largest percentage—55. The Pasis are the next largest community with a population of nearly 34,25,929. This huge dalit population had remained oppressed, repressed, suppressed, and exploited by the Hindu upper castes of UP, sanctioned by their ancient religious texts, for many centuries. However, in the decade of the 1980s, the BSP emerged in UP and succeeded in politically empowering this huge dalit community that had been politically subjugated by the upper caste-led political parties of the state and country. Since its inception, the BSP led by Kumari Mayawati, a 'daughter of dalit', ruled over UP as the leader of the BSP, thus breaking the age-old shackles of the Brahminical order that is still strongly prevalent in this state. In this process the huge dalit community of this state, became a part of the political processes of the country.

The claim of democracy is that it is empowering marginals. In this process, many marginal communities are forming their own political parties to facilitate the process of empowering dalits. For example, through parties such as the RPI and BSP it is believed that their fight is getting strengthened. The victory of the BSP has immensely helped empower the vast sections of dalits and Bahujans (the majority population) of UP who had been languishing on the fringes of democracy with no power to enter into the political processes of the country. However, in this celebration of democracy it is often overlooked that the dalits comprise a large number of castes and communities and of these only a few castes who make up a small section of the total dalit population have acquired visibility, while a huge cluster of dalit communities are still very far from the door of democracy. These castes are still invisible despite the presence of the BSP and continue to remain voiceless and unable to assert themselves for moving ahead. Thus, while the state-led democracy has helped to empower many erstwhile marginalized communities, it also led to the disempowerment of many other small communities. The marginalized communities that have gained power do not want to share it with less fortunate brethren, thus creating a dominant community.

Of the huge heterogeneous dalit community of UP only the Chamar–Pasi twins have succeeded in attaining political visibility; a few castes like the Balmiki, Dhobi, and Koris are fighting to attain visibility, while a large number of smaller castes like Musahar, Bansphor, Sapera, Nat, and so on, are still completely marginalized and not even present in this discourse. Although there are several reasons for the invisibility of the large number of smaller and marginalized dalit castes the major reasons for their multiple invisibility are the absence of their own leadership and consequently not developing a modern politics of their own; absence of education and literacy among them which has led to the non-development of their intellectuals, writers, and journalists who can write and spread information about them and increase their visibility; the small number and scattered form of their population due to which they are unable to conglomerate and make their presence felt during elections; their incapacity to mould their identity in the modern language of politics and power, and so on.

The dalit castes that have progressed are unwilling to share their democratic, political, and socio-economic opportunities and their resources with these marginalized dalit castes who, for their part, have yet to voice aspirations for their basic rights and visibility. They are totally invisible in the Indian state and its welfare schemes. Dalit history and dalit culture in totality are marginalized to a great extent in our country's policies and academic discourses but even within these the history and culture of the marginalized dalit castes are completely absent. The future of the moral and powerful Indian state is completely dependent on how far these marginalized dalit castes are politicized and modernized within the Indian state. As these marginalized dalit castes become politically aware and are able to knock on the doors of democracy, Indian democracy will become stronger and deeper. Many of these original dalit castes are the victims of confusion between how they will negotiate their traditional occupations with the modern state language, and what position they will take regarding education and modern forms of marketing. Their traditional occupations are declining but because they are not familiar with the language and modern politics and development of the state they are unable to make themselves visible in the democratic domain. They are not in the radars of the forces that form the political policies and academic discourses of the country and have not yet been able to haunt their mindspaces. In this book we tried to capture their growing sense of being left out in democracy and democratic representation and their cry for inclusion, which is yet to transform into assertion in the domain of nation, state, democracy, and society. We discussed how during the process of democratization of dalit communities some groups are overrepresented, while many others are still far from the threshold of democracy. These invisible and unseen communities amongst the Dalits are unable to demonstrate their politics of presence in the ever-evolving democracy of UP.

The dalit politics that emerged in UP granted the dalits an identity generated through Bahujan identity politics. This provided many marginalized communities self-confidence, sense of respect, political potential, and helped them attain strength in their struggle for acquiring power. We also understood how some elements of redistributive claims such as issues related to economic marginalization, deprivation, and so on and claims to the politics of recognition, such as cultural domination, dominant visibility, disrespect, humiliation and non-recognition were woven in the Bahujan version of dalit politics in UP. However, in this democratic assertion only a few castes and a small section of dalits acquired visibility and identity while a huge cluster of dalit communities are still very far from the door of democracy and have yet to develop a political identity. This large section remains voiceless and even invisible though the BSP, the party of the dalits and bahujans, has now become an important player in the political playground of India.

The experience of the working of democracy in most parts of the world suggests that there is no escape from identity politics. Democracies throughout the world have their own peculiarities precisely because every nation has its own history, social pulls and pressures. In India, caste is an important social institution that democracy has had to address. The relationship is two-way, each reshaping the other. The complexities deepen as these elements are in constant flux. In the post-colonial society, the space for performative democracy is expanding day by day, and caste identities play an important role. New castes and communities that are entering the democratic sphere are claiming and reclaiming their shares in the power space that facilitates phenomenal growth of identity politics.

In the book we examined whether broader identities like 'dalits', 'Bahujan', and caste identities like 'Chamar', which have emerged as important dalit identity markers, are able to create the sense of sharing political, social, and cultural spaces among the marginal communities of our society. These identity markers create layers of dominance that may or may not be different from the Brahminical forms of domination. Through documenting some narratives about deepening democracy among dalits who exist on the margins we have understood the dalit margins' fear of growing exclusion and further marginalization as a byproduct of democracy at present. We have also tried to map various layers of the sense of excluding others from the sharing of democratic resources by the newly emerged dominant marginal groups, even among their own people, which results in micro inequalities caused by maldistribution of democratic resources.

In the book we also noticed how the identity of the marginal in this competitive democracy that was formed and reshaped and the constituent elements of their identity like caste histories, caste heroes, caste leaders, alternative non-Brahminical popular religion, and so on, is actually working as a 'Brahminical form with a dalit content'. Thus it has remained confined to creating a rupture in Brahminism through Brahminical epistemology. That is why we find a strong caste hierarchy being formed within the dalit communities and the formation of a creamy layer and Brahminical elite among the dalits and the formation of a brahminical middle class among the newly empowered dalits. The reason for this is that the basis of all identity elements (*gunatatva*) is pride in identity based on constant inclusion and exclusion produced on their own desires and feeling of difference with others. These brahminical elements create hierarchy even in the struggle for equalities and constantly produce space for exclusion. In the fight of the dalits for ensuring their space in democracy the elements that add value often create exclusion while asserting exclusiveness.

As an example of the kind of marginalization faced by a marginal dalit community we documented the multiple experience of democracy in north Indian society through the narratives of the Musahar

community of eastern UP. These narratives of multiple marginalizations helped us understand the articulation of democratic experience
by the weaker and marginalized sections of society. We explored how
state-led categories, which had been developed by the state to bring
equality in society, led to the misdistribution of resources and produced marginalization in several cases in Indian society. These articulations of marginalization of small dalit groups may be expressed in
the broader public forum by the intervention of political groups and
NGOs but they emerge through their everyday life in which they
realize the state-led democracy by its presence in the form of various
aspects of social justice.

In this book we tried to explore who are the people who imagine
the(ir) nation. How do the dalits or lower backward castes (especially
the artisan communities called ati dalit) bearing caste-names like
Banjara, Nat, Jogi, Darogas, Rawana, Rajput, Bharbhuja, Pinjara,
Gariya, Luhar, Kachhi, Kasai, Dhobi, Sapera, Baazigar, Khatik,
Darzi, Kumhar, Chhipi, Rangrez, Thatera, Bhishti, and so on, imagine the nation? What is the meaning of the nation-community for
these economically vulnerable and socially marginalized groups?
Concurrently, how do the educated, mainstream dalits (the 'creamy
layer' as the Hinglish jargon goes) with a fair amount of exposure
to the media, imagine the nation? We explored the perception of
the nation among various dalit communities today and studied how
the 'past' circulates among them through the print media, how the
reality-effect of these narratives are generated and nurtured. We also
examined the role that the dalit press plays in transmitting ideas about
the nation. In other words, we tried to show that the communities
that are not exposed to the mainstream media and are not in the
forefront of the competition for 'self-improvement' have a different
story to tell: of the nation, and of themselves.

The marginal castes that are late in historical formation, that is,
have a delayed historical formation, are forming alternative histories

in order to glorify their past and create their identities. However, these histories that are being created by the marginal castes are in the frame of mainstream history and are being formed by castes who are in front and are aware and conscious. Thus the alternative is taking them towards the mainstream. But many castes that do not have their histories are behind these castes and if they form their own history they will take the same path as these castes. The benefit is that they will get an identity that will help them claim a share in democracy but, on the other hand, they will create a dominant and dominated section within themselves. These castes are suffering from democratic deficit because of lack of education, leaders, and so on, and thus their cultural citizenship is not ensured. In the book we examined how the Chamars and Pasis were successful in demarginalizing themselves through the creation of a new history and become a part of mainstream India while the smaller dalit castes that did not follow their path remained behind.

The demarginalization of Dalits in India works on a variety of levels. Through creating new narratives and by virtually inventing a new alternative history and language, this movement, which reached its peak in the decade of the 1980s and 1990s with the formation and growth of the BSP by and under Kanshiram, used a particular style of popular and widely circulated booklets that were avidly read and disseminated by the neo-literate Dalit population. The construction of this alternative history through such new texts, seen as an existential necessity for the Dalits, worked by weaving together stories found in religious Brahminical popular texts about dissenting lower caste characters, glorified as Dalit heroes who fought against upper-caste oppression and injustice. It also included stories of unsung Dalit freedom fighters, transformed into local myths. Importantly, the language used was different from standard hindi, since folk proverbs, idioms and symbols, as well as the grammar and vocabulary of local dialects, were used.

An exploration of the discursive strategies and politics of imagination and narration of the Dalits' own history is helpful in understanding their protests and demands. This goes much deeper than studying politics, though political parties, especially the BSP, have been using these strategies for mobilizing grassroots Dalits, helping them to demand social, economic, and political privileges based on the history of injustice done to them. This complex process of identity reconstruction has a deliberately subversive input in socio-political discourses, providing a strong basis for alternative claims that undermine and challenge the historically grown dominant discourses and combat the everyday humiliation still encountered through largely Brahminical and Sanskritic cultural narratives.

However, as we saw in the book, these processes of constructing new history and culture helped only a few dalit castes like the Chamar and Pasi and, to some extent, Dhobi, Khatik, and Balmiki, to become politically empowered and grab an important place in the political domain of India while smaller dalit castes like Sapera, Nat, Musahar, and so on, have not been able to assert for themselves political space as they do not have an educated and intellectual section that can write their caste histories and make their castes visible. As a result, these castes have remained marginalized among the entire dalit community and are still languishing on the fringes of the dalit fold as a whole.

The meaning of space in democracy is not just limited to providing political representation and economic development to all the communities but also includes providing space to their cultural identities including their dialects. In a state-led democracy all the communities try to acquire visibility and attain cultural citizenship, which helps them to be elevated in the eyes of other castes and get social respect. Cultural citizenship depends on a sense of identity and cultural 'ownership' of each community and extends an invitation to the communities to belong and become a part of democracy.

Cultural citizenship is only realized when there is a sense of authenticity and connection. Sometimes this translates into belonging, and only then is there a recognizable citizenship structure that includes rights and responsibilities. In the book we saw that the invisibility of marginalized dalit castes in India, especially in UP, also extends to their culture and the state-led cultural policies of India, which includes funding, has led to suppression of the culture of dalit castes as a whole, and that among them there is a large section of dalit castes whose culture is invisible even among the other dalit castes, like the Sapera, Nat, Dom, Musahar, Pattharkat, Kanjar, and so on. Most of these castes have their own cultural forms, for example the Doms have their dance called *Dom Kuch*, the Nats have their *Nat Nachna*, while communities like the Musahars and Mahavats have their own linguistic register and own song and dance tradition through which they express their life struggles and so on.

Thus the question I have tried to raise in this book is 'Has this Indian democracy been able to create an equal society since the fight for creating an equal society is producing inequality within itself?' I am not proposing any solution to the problem in the form of the conclusion to this book, but I am trying to identify the problems that may help us critically analyse democracy, state, and movements of assertion in Indian society.

Bibliography

Akela, A.R. (2007). *Kanshi Ram Ke Saakshatkaar*. Delhi: Manak Publication (Pvt.) Limited.

Ambedkar, B.R. (1937). *Yanche Patrak*. Janta, 10 April (Marathi).

Anderson, B. (1991). *Imagined Communities: Reflections on the Origin and Spread of Nationalism* (revised ed.), London and New York: Verso.

Appadurai, A. (1993). 'On "Post-Colonial Discourse"', *The Heart of Whiteness*, 16(4), Special Issue, pp. 796–807.

———. (1997). *Modernity at Large: Cultural Dimensions of Globalization*. New Delhi: Oxford University Press.

———. (2004). 'The Capacity to Aspire: Culture and the Terms of Recognition', in Vijayendra Rao and Michael Walton (eds), *Culture and Public Action*, pp. 59–84. Delhi: Permanent Black.

Barkan, Elazar. (2000). *The Guilt of the Nations: Restitution and Negotiating Historical Injustice*. New York: WW Norton and Company.

Baudh, G.P. (1985). *Buddha ke Baad*. Mathura: Bharti Prakashan.

Bechain, S.S. (1997). *Hindi ki Dalit Patrakarita Par Patrakar Ambedkar ka Prabhav*. New Delhi: Samta Prakashan.

Bhabha, H.K. (1994). *The Location of Culture*. London: Routledge.

Bharti, K. (1997). *Loktantra Mein Bhagidari Ke Sawaal*. Rampur: Bodhisattva Prakashan.

Bourdieu, P. (1990). *The Logic of Practice*. Stanford: Stanford University Press.

Briggs, G.W. (1920). *The Chamars*. Calcutta: Associated Press.

Chakrabarty, D. (2002). 'Museums in Late Democracies: Two Models of Democracy'. *Humanities Research*, 9(1): 5–12.

———. (2002). *Habitations of Modernity: Essays in the Wake of Subaltern Studies*. Delhi: Permanent Black.

———. (2007). 'Minority Histories, Subaltern Pasts', in *Provincializing Europe: Postcolonial Thought and Historical Difference*, pp. 97–113. Princeton: Princeton University Press.

Charsley, S. and Karanth, G.K. (1998). *Challenging Untouchability; Dalit Initiative and Experience from Karnataka: Cultural Subordination and the Dalit Challenge, Volume 1*. New Delhi: Sage Publications.

Chatterjee, P. (2001). 'The Nation in Heterogeneous Time'. *The Indian Economic and Social History Review*, 38(4): 399–418.

———. (2004). *The Politics of the Governed: Reflections on Popular Politics in Most of the World*. New York: Columbia University Press.

Chaudhary, R.K. (1997). *Pasi Samrajya*. Lucknow: Shruti Prakashan.

Choudhary, P. and Shrikant. (2005). *Swarg Par Dhawa: Bihar Mein Dalit Andolan (1912–2000)*. New Delhi: Vani Prakashan.

Coomaraswamy, A. (2006). *The Dance of Siva*. New York: Kessinger Publishing.

Couldry, N. (2010). *Why Voice Matters: Culture and Politics after Neoliberalism*. New Delhi: Sage.

Crook, W. (1968). *Popular Religion and Folklore of Northern India*. New Delhi: Munshiram Manoharlal.

Davies, S. (2003). *Empiricism and History*. New York: Palgrave Macmillan.

Derrida, J. (1973). *Speech and Phenomena and Other Essays on Husserl's Theory of Signs*, translated by D.B. Allison and N. Garver. Evanston: Northwestern University Press.

Devika, J. (2013). 'Contemporary Dalit Assertions in Kerala: Governmental Categories vs. Identity Politics?' *History and Sociology of South Asia*, 7(1): 1–17.

Devy, G.N., V. Geoffrey, and K.K. Chakravarty (eds). (2013). *Narrating Nomadism: Tales of Recovery and Resistance*, pp. 1–12. New Delhi: Routledge.

Dirks, N.B. (2001). *Castes of Mind: Colonialism and the Making of Modern India*. Princeton: Princeton University Press.

———— (2002). *Castes of Mind: Colonialism and the Making of Modern India*. Delhi: Permanent Black.

Dwivedi, H.P. (2008). *Kabir*. New Delhi: Rajkamal Prakashan.

Foucault, M. (1977). 'Nietzche, Genealogy, History', translated by Donald F. Bouchard and Sherry Simon in Donald F. Bouchard (ed.), *Michel Foucault: Language, Counter-Memory, Practice: Selected Essays and Interviews*, pp. 139–64. Ithaca, NY: Cornell University Press.

Fraser, Nancy. (1996). *Social Justice in the Age of Identity Politics: Redistribution, Recognition and Participation*. The Tanner Lecture on Human Values, 30 April–2 May.

Gooptu, N. (2006). *Swami Acchutanand and the Adi Hindu Movement*. New Delhi: Cambridge University Press.

Gordon, D. (1995). 'Review of Patrick H. Hutton: History as an Art of Memory'. *History and Theory*, 34(4): 340–54.

Government of India. (1994–5). Report of the High Powered Committee Appointed by the Ministry of Human Resource Development to Review the Seven Zonal Cultural Centres.

Grierson, G.A. (1975). *Bihar Peasant Life: Being a Discursive Catalogue*. New Delhi: Cosmo Publication.

Hacking, I. (1975). *The Emergence of Probability: A Philosophical Study of Early Ideas about Probability, Induction and Statistical Inference*. Cambridge: Cambridge University Press.

Hacking, I. (1986). 'Making Up People', in Thomas O. Heller, et al. (eds), *Reconstructing Individualism: Autonomy, Individuality and the Self in Western Thought*, pp. 222–36. Stanford, CA: Stanford University Press.

Hans, B.S. (2003). *Gau Brahmin Namo-Namo, Ko Rakshati Vedah*. Patna: Ambedkar Mission Prakashan.

Hermes, J. and R. Adolfsson. (2007). 'The (Multiple) Realities of Cultural Citizenship', paper presented at Shifting Politics, Groningen University, June.

Hoare, Q. and G.N. Smith. (1996). *Selections from the Prison Notebooks of Antonio Gramsci* (ed. and trans.). New Delhi: Samya Publications.

Hoy, D. Couzens. (1986). 'Introduction', in David Counzens Hoy (ed.), *Foucault: A Critical Reader*, pp. 1–25. Oxford: Basil Blackwell.

Human Development Report. (2004). 'Cultural Liberty in Today's Diverse World'. New Delhi: Oxford University Press.

Illaiah, K. (1996). *Why I Am Not a Hindu: A Sudra Critique of Hindutva Philosophy, Culture and Political Economy.* Kolkata: Samya Publications.

Jain, J. (2000). 'Indian "Folk Art" Tradition, Revival and Transformation', in P. Pal (ed.), *Reflections on the Arts in India*, pp. 61–71. Mumbai: India Marg Publications.

Jenkins, L.D. (2003). *Identity and Identification in India: Defining the Disadvantaged.* London and New York: Routledge Curzon.

Jha, D.N. (1998). *Ancient India: A Historical Outline.* New Delhi: Manohar.

Joshi, H. and S. Kumar. (2002). *Asserting Voices: Changing Culture, Identity and Livelihood of the Musahars in the Gangetic Plains.* New Delhi: Deshkaal Publications.

Kaviraj, S. (1993). 'The Imaginary Institution of India', in Partha Chatterjee and Gyanendra Pandey (eds), *Subaltern Studies 7*, pp. 1–40. New Delhi: Oxford University Press.

———. (2005). *On the Enchantment of the State: Indian Thought on the Role of the State in the Narrative of Modernity.* London: SOAS.

Kolenda, P. (1978). *Caste in Contemporary India: Beyond Organic Solidarity.* Menlo Park: Benjamin/Cummings.

Kshirsagar, R.K. (1994). *Dalit Movement in India and Its Leaders.* Delhi: M.D. Publication.

Kumar, V. and U. Sinha. (2001). *Dalit Assertion and Bahujan Samaj Party: A Perspective from Below.* Lucknow: Bahujan Sahitya Sansthan.

Kushwaha, C.L. (ed.) (1996). *Kanshiram: Press ke Saamne.* Allahabad: Kushwaha Publication.

Kushwaha, S.C. (1993). *Arakshan ke Hatyare.* Allahabad: Kushwaha Publication.

Lynch, O.M. (1974). *The Politics of Untouchability.* New Delhi: National Publishing House.

Majumder, D.N. (1941). *The Fortunes of Primitive Tribes.* Lucknow: Universal Publishers Ltd.

Marriott, A. (2003). 'Dalit or Harijan? Self-Naming by Scheduled Caste Interviewees'. *Economic and Political Weekly*, XXXVIII(36): 3741–831.

Marx, K. (1992). *Surveys from Exile*, trans. David Fernbach. New York: Vintage.

Nagendra, S.P. (2012). 'Towards a Cultural Policy in India: Can Culture Be Planned?', in Lakshmanna and Jugendra Sahai (eds), *Society and Culture*. New Delhi: Rawat Publications.

Nandy, A. (2003). *The Romance of the State and the Fate of Dissent in the Tropics*. New Delhi: Oxford University Press.

Narayan, B. (2001). *Documenting Dissent: Contesting Fables, Contested Memories and Dalit Political Discourse*. Shimla: Indian Institute of Advanced Study.

———. (2004). 'Inventing Caste Histories: Dalit Mobilisation and Nationalist Past'. *Contributions to Indian Sociology*, 38(1–2): 193–220.

———. (2006). *Women Heroes and Dalit Assertion in North India: Culture, Identity and Politics*. New Delhi: Sage Publications.

Navsarjan Trust and Robert F. Kennedy Center for Justice and Human Rights. (2009). *Understanding Untouchability: A Comprehensive Study of Practices and Conditions in 1589 Villages*.

Norris, C. (1992). *Deconstruction: Theory and Practice*. London: Routledge.

Omvedt, G. (1996). *Dalit Vision: The Anti-caste Movement and the Construction of an Indian Identity*. Delhi: Orient Longman.

Pandey, G.C. (2006). 'The Subaltern as Subaltern Citizen'. *Economic and Political Weekly*, November 18, 41(46): 4735–41.

Pawan, R. (1992). *Tanda Kisan Andolan: Krantikari Goodar Ram*. Bahraich: Lakshya Sandhan Prakashan [Lakshya Sandhan Booklet Series, 9].

Pieterse, J.N. (2004). *The Cultural Turn: Questions of Power, Development Theory: Deconstructions/ Reconstructions*. New Delhi: Vistaar Publications.

Prasad, M. (1995). *Uttar Pradesh ki Dalit Jatiyon ka Dastavej*. New Delhi: Kitab Ghar.

———. (2007). *Uttaranchal Sahit Uttar Pradesh ki Dalit Jaatiyon ka Dastavaej*. New Delhi: Samyak Prakashan.

Prashant, G.P. (1994). *Mool Vansha Katha*. Lucknow: Cultural Publishers.

Ram, Nandu. (1995). *Beyond Ambedkar: Essays on Dalits in India*. New Delhi: Har Anand Publications.

Rao, V. and M. Walton. (2004). *Culture and Public Action*. New Delhi: Permanent Black.

Rathore, A.S. and A. Verma (eds). (2011). *B.R. Ambedkar the Buddha and His Dhamma: A Critical Edition*. New Delhi: Oxford University Press.

Sagar, M.P. (1987). *Achhut Virangana*. Lucknow: Cultural Publishers.

Sankrityayan, R. (1993). *Pali Sahitya ka Itihas*. Delhi: Vani Prakashan.

Saran, B.H. (1998). *Kash Hum Hindu Na Hote*. Chitkohara, Patna: Ambedkar Mission Prakashan.

Sen, A. (1999). *Development as Freedom*. Oxford: Oxford University Press.

Seneviratne, H.L. (ed.) (1997). *Identity, Consciousness and Past*. New Delhi: Oxford University Press.

Singh, K.S. (1995). *People of India*, National Series Volume II, The Scheduled Castes. New Delhi: Oxford University Press.

———. (ed.) (2005). *People of India: Uttar Pradesh (Anthropological Survey of India)*, vol. XLII, parts 1–3. New Delhi: Manohar Publishers.

Singh, R.K. (1994). *Kanshiram aur BSP*. Allahabad: Kushwaha Publications.

Singh, Ramashankar. (2015). 'Bansor, Baans Aur Loktantra'. *Pratimaan*, 3(1): 255–72.

Sinha, A. (2007). 'Tenure Ends but No Report from Cultural Panel', *Indian Express*, 3 May 2007.

Spivak, G.C. (1988). 'Can the Subaltern Speak?' in Cary Nelson and Larry Grossberg (eds), *Marxism and the Interpretation of Culture*, pp. 271–313. Chicago: University of Illinois Press.

Stewart, F. (2009). *A Global View of Horizontal Inequalities: Inequalities Experienced by Muslims Worldwide*. Microcon Research Working Paper 13. Brighton: Microcon.

Tanabe, A. (2007). *American Ethnologist. Toward Vernacular Democracy: Moral Society and Post-Colonial Transformation in Rural Orissa, India*. Kyoto University: Institute for Research in Humanities.

Thurston, E. and K. Rangachari. (1909). *Castes and Tribes of Southern India*. Madras: Government Press.

Turner, B.S. (ed.). (1990). *Theories of Modernity and Postmodernity*. London: Sage.

Valmiki, O.P. (1997). *Joothan*. Delhi: Vani Prakashan.

Varma, B.L. [1951] (1991). 'Jhansi Ki Rani', in *Brindavan Lal Varma Samagra*, pp. 814–95, vol. 3. Varanasi: Hindi Granthalaya.

Vatsyayan, K.M. (1972). *Some Aspects of Cultural Policies in India*. Paris: UNESCO.

Venkata Siva Reddy, G. (2002). 'Competition and Conflict among the Dalits: Madiga Dandora Movement in Andhra Pradesh', in G.S. Shah (ed.), *Dalits and the State*, pp. 325–42. New Delhi: Concept Publishing Company.

Zelliot, E. (2001). *From Untouchable to Dalit: Essays on the Ambedkar Movement*. New Delhi: Manohar.

Index

About the Author

Badri Narayan is a social historian and cultural anthropologist. He is currently Professor at the Centre for the Study of Discrimination and Exclusion, School of Social Sciences, Jawaharlal Nehru University, New Delhi. His wide-ranging interests cover culture, memory, and politics, contemporary histories, ethnography of marginalized politics, social and anthropological history, dalit and subaltern issues, and identity formation and the question of power. He was a recipient of the Fulbright Senior Fellowship (September 2005–April 2006) and the Smuts Fellowship, University of Cambridge (February 2007–October 2007). He has been a Fellow at the Indian Institute of Advanced Study, Shimla (1998–9), Visiting Fellow at the International Institute of Asian Studies, University of Leiden, The Netherlands (2002), and HGIS Fellow at the Royal Tropical Institute, Amsterdam (2001). Besides having written a number of articles in both English and Hindi, he has authored *Kanshiram: Leader of the Dalits* (2014), *The Making of the Dalit Public in North India: Uttar Pradesh, 1950–Present* (Oxford University Press, 2011), *Fascinating Hindutva: Saffron Politics and Dalit Mobilisation* (2009), *Women Heroes and Dalit Assertion in North India* (2006),

Documenting Dissent: Contesting Fables, Contested Memories and Dalit Political Discourse (2001). He has also completed various national and international projects successfully.

He has been the Coordinator of Dalit Resource Centre, a centre established by his active efforts funded by the Ford Foundation at the GB Pant Social Science Institute, Jhusi, Allahabad. Due to his academic and literary contributions, he has been the recipient of many prestigious literary awards like the Mira Smriti Puraskaar (2012), Shamsher Samman (2012), Spandan Kriti Samman (2010), Kedar Samman (2006), and Banarasi Prasad Bhojpuri Samman (2002).